westland ltd

# I, Me and Us:
## Insights of an Ex-Schizophrenic

Ganesh N. Rajan is an engineering graduate with an MBA in International Business and Master's in Social and Applied Economics from Ohio, USA. He has been a consultant in various capacities in the USA, India and Japan since 1993.

Ganesh was afflicted with schizophrenia, in his late teens. He went through the entire cycle of the disability, and, over a three-year sabbatical, he was able to tackle the condition. Over time, he developed the ability to keep schizophrenic symptoms in remission, using an assortment of hypotheses and heuristics.

In *I, Me and Us*, Ganesh's first full-length book, refined over fifteen years, he shares the ideas that continue to help him manage his condition. Because of an innate sensitivity, and from probing into his own mind's functioning, he ended up with original insights on social interaction. Ganesh challenges popular but flawed beliefs, which often cause dissatisfaction and unhappiness. The insights he shares in *I, Me and Us* can reorient the vulnerable, and help many of the conventionally 'normal' others acquire a sense of fulfilment.

Ganesh is currently engaged in business process consulting, creative-writing assignments and patient-to-patient (P2P)™ counselling, based out of Chennai, India.

# Praise for the Author

'I have read many first person accounts of the experiences that people have gone through when they've been afflicted by the most devastating of psychiatric disorders—Schizophrenia. But, in all truth, I've never read one like *I, Me and Us*. What makes it so special, are the insights that Ganesh, the author, has not merely obtained, but also shared with such lucidity to anyone who reads this wonderful book. What's most interesting is that the insights are not limited merely to surviving the illness, but have to do with life and the cognitive experience itself. Well structured, crisp and clear, the book can help anyone looking for a roadmap to manoeuvre their ways around the speed bumps and potholes that our lives today encounter. It's a terrific read and one that I would recommend to all those who are looking for some anchor points with which to navigate life's vagaries.'
— Dr. Vijay Nagaswami – Psychiatrist and Bestselling Author

'*I, Me and Us* is written by a person who has had to contend with a major psychiatric disorder in the best years of his life, and yet has managed to lead a meaningful existence with a good work record, a family, and a zest to share his life experiences. This book epitomises the fact that persons with major mental disorders can attain a state of normality comparable to others. This is well in keeping with the concept of recovery that is being targeted all over the world as a desirable outcome. While those with schizophrenia and their family members will probably identify with the experiences recounted in the narrative, this isn't all the book has to offer. As the author himself mentions, he has spoken of philosophy, psychology and self-help. You will therefore find tips to

cope with mental illness interlaced with philosophical and existential themes in a very intriguing and interesting manner.'
—Dr R Thara, Director: Schizophrenia Research Foundation (SCARF), Chennai, India.

'Schizophrenia is one of the most devastating mental illnesses anyone can encounter. Suffering from this disorder and coming to terms with it, gaining insight to the illness, continuing medication and ultimately triumphing over this malady is not something easy to achieve. Ganesh Rajan has achieved this rather difficult feat with great aplomb... This book is in the form of a narrative about the illness, the process and recovery, with an emphasis on adherence to medication, while it also has a lot of self-analysis by the author. This narration will surely help on how to cope with this problem... He has written this volume under various chapters with a liberal sprinkling of supporting insights from diverse sources. It speaks volumes of his erudition and depth of knowledge, not only in what he is trying to convey, but also his knowledge in the field of literature.'
—Dr S. Kalyanasundaram, Hon. CEO: Richmond Fellowship Society & Professor of Psychiatry and Principal: RF PG College for Psychosocial Rehabilitation, Bengaluru, India.

# I, Me and Us

## Insights of an Ex-Schizophrenic

GANESH N. RAJAN

**westland ltd**

61, II Floor, Silverline Building, Alapakkam Main Road,
Maduravoyal, Chennai 600095
93, I Floor, Sham Lal Road, Daryaganj, New Delhi 110002

First published by westland ltd 2015

Copyright © Ganesh Natarajan 2015

All rights reserved

10 9 8 7 6 5 4 3 2 1

ISBN: 978-93-85152-13-9

Typeset by PrePSol Enterprises Pvt. Ltd.

I dedicate this book to my wife, Kalpana, my parents, my children, my siblings, and the rest of my family, immediate and extended.
Thank you for giving me extraordinary support and understanding.

# Table of Contents

# PREFACE

What are the shareable insights an ex-schizophrenic can have? As a person with schizophrenia, I felt unequipped to face life. I woke up to a world playing various games loaded with discouraging psychosocial measures and rules. Even people who seemed normal appeared to me as wrestling ineffectively with their situation. Some seemed to have severe hang-ups from the past. Others constantly compared their lot with those around them. Yet others read a deceptively mystical twist in their reality. Going through schizophrenia opened my eyes to the importance of having a practical and real personal purpose. Several insights helped me towards acquiring a more proactive, confident and poised disposition. I feel the revelations I stumbled upon, and built on, are too valuable to keep confined to myself.

Why aren't there books that can reassure and teach us that one can succeed without having to be the best of the best? Why are people obsessed with measuring their success against that of others? Why do cues from our environment appear to promote such a relative success? Why do some succumb to superstition and the surreal in thought, word and deed? Where are the answers for the millions who live modestly, going from challenge to challenge, just living? As a response to such questions, I have tried to explore a broad, all-encompassing objective: How can anyone truly belong in the process called life? I have strived to do justice to this broad and ambitious intent despite my limitations. The result is this book.

*I, Me and Us* uses schizophrenia as a framework to explore many kinds of negativity—in both the ostensibly sane, and the obviously afflicted. The book has a generous dose of prescriptive and generic advice. In it, I explore some ideas and techniques that can help each of us recognise our own uniqueness, and, become proactive in our approach. I go over Creation, interaction, and gumption from fresh perspectives.

In the attempt to be comprehensive, I think I have thrown in everything but the kitchen-sink into the book. A kitchen-sink in context, which you may notice as missing, is an explanation for pointless pain: Pain and suffering that is neither an alarm nor a teacher or part of an addressable mission. Such issues, I am saving to ask of the Big One!

✳ ✳ ✳

Schizophrenia is a much-misunderstood condition. According to statistics, schizophrenia affects 1 per cent of the population at some point in their lives. This condition is independent of nationality, social or economic status, religion and gender. Most people confuse it with multiple personality disorder, but schizophrenia is different. Schizophrenia appears to be a mental manifestation of a physical condition. The symptoms of schizophrenia are of two kinds—positive and negative. The positive symptoms are those that should not be present but are, such as delusions and hallucinations. A hallucination may be auditory, visual, tactile or olfactory and is a sensory perception without any stimulus. Delusion is a false, fixed belief. Persons with schizophrenia hold on to it with such conviction that logical reasoning or evidence to the contrary is unable to shake it.

Negative symptoms of schizophrenia are called as such because they are related to behaviours absent in afflicted persons, but normally found in healthy individuals; symptoms which reflect the loss or absence of normal traits or abilities. Common negative symptoms are flat or blunted emotion, poverty of speech, inability to experience pleasure, lack of desire to form relationships, and lack of motivation. While medication can alleviate the positive symptoms of schizophrenia, the negative symptoms often remain. This could prevent persons with schizophrenia from getting back into the social mainstream.

Dr RD Laing (1927–87) was a noted British psychiatrist, known for his out-of-the-box thinking. He blamed society's unliveable condition for the rise of schizophrenia and other mental illnesses. Marshall McLuhan (1911–80), a prominent Canadian communications theorist, suggested, 'Schizophrenia maybe a necessary consequence (sic) of literacy.' Some claim 'stress-diathesis,' a combination of stress and dormant triggers, causes the illness. I subscribe to theories that suggest reasons for the onset are psychological or psychosocial, in addition to the physiological. I hence feel that empathising with the afflicted person and applying tactful nudges towards reality can prevent aggravation or bring about enduring remission. I think that with willingness and a push towards normality, many can acquire a sense of wellness, and come back to mainstream social life.

✳ ✳ ✳

A fictional dialogue with a young person having schizophrenia precedes all chapters, save the last one. This preamble to each chapter is entirely fabricated, and primarily a device introduced to thread the book's concepts. I portray the person with schizophrenia as articulate, despite his illness. Furthermore, the maverick therapeutic approach and rapid recovery depicted are atypical. I wrote, with a great degree of literary licence, to be generic and relevant to a diverse audience. I must also apologise upfront for playing fast and loose with the terms schizophrenic, affliction, disability, patient and the like, using the same licence. Many are still trying to sort out the stigma and negative connotations of such terms. I want to add to the awareness and understanding of mental illness, and perhaps prevent onset, not compound any confusion.

*I, Me and Us* is an eclectic combination of philosophy, psychology and self-help. It is, in some ways, an attempt to define what is sane and successful. We know sanity and success, but they elude a straightjacketed definition. Regardless of what and who you are, you will hopefully discover a sense of success, sanity and wellness by considering the book's concepts. While it is hard to be generic and still address individual problems, *I, Me and Us*, I believe, has enough information to help everybody. Don't think *I don't have schizophrenia, so this is not for me.* Throughout the work, I have used the pronoun 'He' for convenience, but schizophrenia does not discriminate, and the references are equally applicable to both genders.

I experienced a growth exceeding expectations as I articulated the ideas in the book. My maturity in taking what life can dish out, my ability to be proactive and my capacity to be patient, all grew significantly. Yet, I feel the true example of its lessons is a person that I have only glimpsed in my mind's eye. Such a person, more often than not, would be able to apply the information and solutions shared in the book effortlessly and effectively to life. In *I, Me and Us,* 'I' is the individual, 'Me' is the package of desires, limitation and tendencies of the individual, and 'Us' is the interaction of this package with the environment. I hope, in its own small way, *I, Me and Us* will help demystify life, and make our world a better place. If some explanations in the book seem radical, just enjoy the irreverence. Don't shoot the messenger! My goal is to be helpful to the greatest number, to the greatest feasible degree. Read on!

Ganesh N. Rajan
February 2015, India.

# PART I: The Problem

I built on an illustration shared in a publication for children, and put together the following anecdote: A missionary in the Africa of a long time ago sent a native to another mission in a neighbouring village to borrow a hammer. The missionary made the native wear a wooden plaque around his neck. It had the words, 'SEND HAMMER' burnt into the wood. The native went to the neighbouring village, was given the hammer at the mission and returned with it. The native was convinced the spell carved on the plaque had made spirits talk and ask for the hammer. The missionary tried to explain that no spirits had talked and that the spell was actually language. The native answered, 'If it talks without speaking, it is a spirit.'

# INTROSPECTION

The parents seemed unsure where to start. Dr Dharmaraj, the psychiatrist, opened the discussion by asking some general questions about the family to put them at ease. Then, when he asked if there had been any out-of-the-ordinary behaviour, it was like turning on a tap.

Nachiket was a nineteen-year-old youth. Now, Nachiket was under the delusion that he was the mythical Nachiketa reborn. The doctor knew of the Hindu mythological tale in which a father makes an offering of his son, Nachiketa, to Yama, the God of death and justice.

The mythical Nachiketa's father, Vaajasravas, was a very strict practitioner of Hindu rituals. He performed a *yagna*[1], as part of which he gave away cows in ritualistic compensation. These cows found it difficult even to eat grass or drink water, leave alone yield milk! They were

---

[1]    An event of communal offering in the Hindu religion

too old for any useful purpose. Seeing this, his virtuous and intelligent son, Nachiketa, foresaw a great deal of sorrow for his father because of the flawed offerings. Nachiketa wanted to save Vaajasravas from this fate. To shock his father into seeing sense, the boy asked to whom he intended to offer his own son as a gift. He pestered Vaajasravas to give him away to someone as well. At this, Vaajasravas got so annoyed that he declared in disgust, 'I am giving you to the God of Death.' Nachiketa then resolved that he must make his father's words come true, though they were uttered in anger. Nachiketa persuaded his father to offer him as a gift to Yama, in strict ritualistic style. The story goes that Yama, impressed by Nachiketa's fearlessness, gave him three boons. As one of the boons, Nachiketa asked for the ability to understand if a mortal exists after death and how. The ensuing dialogue between Yama and Nachiketa, prompted by this question, forms the focal point of the Hindu scripture known as the *Kathopanishad*.

Our fictional patient, the delusional Nachiket, was a timid and shy person. However, lately he would have intense outbursts for no apparent reason. He had been furiously reading various scriptures and philosophical texts for the previous six weeks, ignoring everything else. He hadn't slept or eaten much in the past two weeks and was answering all questions in monosyllables. The past two nights, he had just kept awake. Now he refused to speak, communicating only with a nod or by shaking his head. He had stalled all attempts by his parents to take him to a doctor. The only reason he had agreed now seemed to be that the doctor's name was Dharmaraj. Dharmaraj is another name for Yama, in his role as the dispenser of ultimate justice.

Nachiket's parents had built-up on the doctor's name to lure him into a meeting, even implying the possibility of the doctor's divinity. The parents looked pleadingly at the doctor and suggested that if he went along with their son's delusion, Dharmaraj could persuade the youth to talk. The depth of this delusion was so immense that to do otherwise seemed a dead end. The doctor asked the parents to send in Nachiket. The boy's eyes were wild, but he seemed sure of himself, and willingly started to talk. The doctor realised, a few seconds into the conversation that this role play was going to be more taxing than he had anticipated.

'You are Dharmaraj, right?' Nachiket asked.

'Yes,' the doctor replied, glad that Nachiket had framed his question in such a manner that he did not have to lie.

'So you must know why I am here,' Nachiket continued.

'Yes, I do, but I would like to hear it from you,' said the doctor, still hedging.

Nachiket then launched into an excited outburst, taking for granted that Dharmaraj was divine, 'First, I thank you, Lord of Dharma, for all you have shared in my previous birth regarding the afterlife. I still have some questions, not about the afterlife, but about life itself. Many questions have bothered humankind in the past and continue to do so even today—of self and soul, of existence, and the human-animal distinction too. It seems the singular ability of language sets me apart from animals. How am I able to understand you, and how will I carry this understanding forward?'

The doctor took a deep breath before answering, pondering the ethical implications of continuing in this manner. 'You understand me because we were created to understand each other. The human species alone, in all of creation has the gift of language and the ability to communicate complex spoken and written notions. Language enables us to understand each other, and to carry the understanding forward.'

Nachiket continued, quite unabashedly, 'Does this mean I can convey to another, as lucidly as you have conveyed to me, the subjects we have explored?'

Dharmaraj decided to get into the role as earnestly as possible. If he could guide Nachiket out of his delusion, it would be a breakthrough, even if it was an unorthodox approach. 'Soon humanity will have instruments that make it possible to reproduce accurately any communication by another human. These instruments of the future will be able to record interactions in a manner unknown today. They will capture every word, every inflexion, and every visible action humans perform, in glorious three-dimensionality. This will certainly enhance communication.'

'That is so wonderful!' exclaimed Nachiket. 'This means every human will understand exactly the way I have, as I will be able to reproduce my experience and understanding exactly. I hear voices, see symbols, and smell things that no one else apparently can. I believe you have granted me these powers for a purpose.'

Dharmaraj then attempted to introduce a real focus gently. 'Each of us sees and understands creation based on personal experience. At the core of understanding is a unique self, qualifying all meaningful stimulation one receives. Some of the perceived stimuli may even be your own metaphorical mental projections of flawed experiences and learning.'

Nachiket responded with another question, 'What is it that determines how each person understands something, independent of the message itself? Is it the message or our understanding of it that is flawed?'

Dharmaraj then spoke about the learning of the human species. 'We are independent conscious beings in some respects; and connected to the species in some others. This connectivity therefore extends a person's learning beyond specific personal experience. What one understands depends on a collective learning of the species as well as the individual's own independent learning. Both kinds of learning may be helpful or flawed, as well as subtle or gross.'

Nachiket was full of questions. 'Will we ever know what is damaging our understanding, so that we can take corrective action?'

Dharmaraj answered, 'Some of this is sewn into your very being, and can only be experienced. It comes to you as a disposition—a learning that you have no control over. It exists, as much as we exist as a species. The good news is any damaging impact can be managed with effort and a personal willingness to change.'

'Do I have this learning of my species in me?' Nachiket asked.

Dharmaraj tried to describe the species' learning as he confirmed Nachiket's query. 'Surely, you do. A part of the learning is mechanical, but a part of it is moderated through the unique ability we possess as a human species—that of language. This brings us back to your earlier question: how do you understand my ideas and me? I have to answer, it is by your conscious recognition of patterns, such as language—over which you have some control, and by an inner witness that determines your reaction to the patterns—over which you may have limited or no control at all.'

Nachiket was keen to know more. 'Is there a common way in which the inner witness reacts for all of us?'

The doctor chose his words carefully. 'You have some mental repositories in which some patterns become residual. Our background and experience imprints these residual patterns long before we acquire the capability to judge them as right or wrong. These include impressions of forces like culture, local adaptations, tradition, or language and race. The reactions of different people will be similar to the extent of their having shared origins. These impressions guide us, before we acquire the ability to decide independently.

You could become aware of such repositories and your ability to exercise choice when you are a child, a youth, or an older person. When you get to realise you can choose independently, you could perceive the situation you are in as woeful or favourable, or, a whole range of states in-between. In this is the test of the mortal. One can see oneself as an evolving being from the point we awake to our reality, or adversely, as thrown into the vicissitudes of living. Let me ask you—do you feel awake or asleep, disadvantaged or in control?'

Nachiket provided another clue on his mental state and paranoid condition, 'I feel others can read my mind and are hiding a special knowledge from me. This is why I came to you.'

'Can you write what you feel and bring it to me?' The doctor asked, knowing that keeping a journal, though difficult, would help Nachiket focus.

'I will try to do that,' Nachiket answered. 'So many ideas and voices crowd my head.'

'Let us meet again… Okay?' The doctor concluded. 'I am writing down some pills for you to take in the meantime. These should help you with clearing up your head.'

'I will take it as *prasad*[2],' said Nachiket reverently.

Dr Dharmaraj called in the parents, gave them his preliminary diagnosis of schizophrenia, and explained the condition. He also explained that recovery might take a while, as it usually needs a few trials to get the medication right, if at all. Different people seem to require different medication, or combinations of medicines, and also, require different dosage levels, though they may display similar symptoms. Conversely, insight may be swift and facilitate quick recovery. Medication is often lifelong, but then again, sometimes is required only for a short while. For the time being, the doctor advised the parents to avoid confronting Nachiket, or to pander to his delusions. The doctor was glad that Nachiket was not one of those persons that refused medication.

## THE COMMON CONFUSION

The human species is at the pinnacle of the evolutionary pyramid. Yet, many people seem adrift in their worlds. Some people experience odd happenings that conflict

---

[2]    Blessed and holy food in Hinduism

with rational thought. Nachiket was one such individual. He found himself in a contorted reality that begged new explanations. Professionals classify the experiences of a person with schizophrenia, such as hallucinations and delusions, as only superficial symptoms of a deeper physical malaise. These symptoms however appear tangible and real to the experiencer. The person experiences a personal reality that is perplexing and demands a new approach. He could attempt to force-fit, unsuccessfully, the oddities he perceives using only the knowledge he presently has. An afflicted person may imaginatively link up unconnected trivia and overlay spurious meanings onto the inane. The behaviour resulting from such attempts will seem bizarre to a 'normal' observer.

Normal people, in the commonly understood sense of normality, may also experience obscure dark phases. This 'darkness' occurs when the knowledge they possess

> For some, new paradigms may trigger timidity, fear, anxiety and other such negatives.

is insufficient to handle what they face, as in the case of afflicted people. When faced with a new environment, a special relationship or a different philosophy, a normal person could slip into a milder form of unhelpful thinking too. For some, new paradigms may trigger timidity, fear, anxiety and other such negatives. A shortfall in learning may almost force some people to be irrational, unreasonable or aggressive in their attempts to strike a balance. Since reality is, in several ways, different from whatever theory can explain, some people may gradually descend into damaging thinking.

Schizophrenia is more likely among those who adopt a 'limiting ideology' to live by, rather than those who keep an open mind. Limiting ideologies are closed and introverted beliefs, mostly remnants from the past. They keep a person in a comfortable, seemingly normal, but artificial cocoon. Such ideologies typically gloss over practical realities. When stress triggers a strange sensitivity, the person could perceive a private reality which is inexplicable. With growing distress, an invasive environment unlike anything the individual has experienced before could get unveiled. Some have the onset of mental disabilities like schizophrenia. The overly sensitive, even when 'normal' otherwise, could also retreat psychologically and become diffident or aggressive.

Why are some people more sensitive than others? What are the forces that turn a sensible child into an insecure adult? What made Nachiket look to mythology for

> In both afflicted and normal individuals, the learning acquired thus far by the person is unable to explain a new experience.

answers? How can the experiences of a person who went through schizophrenia help normal people? Where is the parallel with schizophrenia? The parallel may be a lack of key foundational knowledge in both, the persons with schizophrenia and other normal people. In both afflicted and normal individuals, the learning acquired thus far by the person is unable to explain a new experience. A feeling of being inadequate can cause reactive or unreasonable behaviour in anyone. This is the 'common confusion' in both the afflicted and normal.

As we go further on into the book, the fictional Dr Dharmaraj implies there are four problems holding us back from functioning effectively. Firstly, flawed theoretical explanations, especially on competition and winning. Secondly, the impact of faulty corporal, lingual or other symbolic cues in transactions amongst people; this includes hallucinations and surreal meanings as experienced in schizophrenia. Thirdly, social pressure that fosters, what we will eventually argue are, misplaced desires for us to be superior in aspects such as abilities and possessions. Finally, the trauma of being born is our fourth problem. Human birth might be the greatest original traumatic experience an individual undergoes. The change in environment from the womb to the outside world is shocking. This trauma of birthing is likely to have influenced our early actions and experiences, some of which could have been harmful. Explanations for these problems, and advice on how to cope with them, could help you be more poised, proactive and productive. It did for me, in the course of my writing and applying the book's concepts.

You are reading this book after making a conscious decision to do it. You read this, and make sense of the words you are reading. This is impossible for any other primate. Then again, is the human species all that special? Many still carry out uncivilised and barbaric acts. Can anyone genuinely validate that we are a civilised society? Can any one person tell others how they should be? This book ambitiously asserts that there are explanations for *all that is* in creation. It is emphatic in claiming we can resolve many factors that cause adverse feelings. The book should help you in overcoming oppressive elements, and much of our inner conflict. It would also help in alleviating feelings of being a victim in

> Those who find a
> deeper purpose can feel,
> and make a difference.

an unfair, unjust environment. Those who find a deeper purpose can feel, and make a difference. Give your *I, Me and Us* a chance to accept being (in the) here (and the) now. Be willing. The rest is relatively easy.

### *Section Highlights:*

- A sense of inadequacy is behind a wide range of damaging thinking for both the afflicted and normal.
- Persons with schizophrenia lack explanations for the symptoms they experience and hence may adopt spurious reasoning.
- We can derive lessons from schizophrenic experiences to overcome much of our unproductive thinking.
- We can nullify common aberrations such as fear, timidity, anxiety, discontent, etc., through these lessons.
- The aberrations can be nullified by understanding the four problems of faulty theory, incorrect symbolic cues, misplaced social pressures and the trauma of human birth.

## SUFFERING SYMBOLISM

Consider that schizophrenia may be a consequence of literacy—an observation made by Marshall McLuhan

(1911–80), a prominent Canadian communications theorist. What is the genesis of literacy? How did we humans become literate in the first place, flaws and all? Let us briefly indulge in pop-Darwinism. There is a hypothesis that the division of the human brain into right and left hemispheres could be a result of evolution. The hypothesis suggests that humans gradually mutated to have this division as a backup. Our fledgling species was helped by such a backup to survive cranial damage from events such as a falling rock or the jaws of a predator[3]. Subsequently, the existence of this 'spare' brain enabled specialisation within each hemisphere. Unlike other species with dual hemispherical brains, this backup lent itself to something more for us humans because of its size, neuron density and the availability of abundant energy from easily digestible cooked food. Cooking allowed us to ingest a lot of calories in a much shorter time as opposed to other species having to forage, hours on end. This also left us sufficient time to carry out other activities, and for our intellect to develop[4].

According to the theory of evolution, whenever a minor change in a being's physiology aids its survival, this change is emphasised. This continues until it is full-blown or until it loses its importance as a survival tool.

---

[3]    Joel Achenbach; Why Things Are: Answers to Every Essential Question in Life; New York: Ballantine Books; 1991.

[4]    This is a novel idea proposed by Suzana Herculano-Houzel, an associate professor at the Federal University of Rio de Janeiro, Brazil, For more information, please visit:   http://www.ted.com/talks/suzana_herculano_houzel_what_is_so_special_about_the_human_brain

The human right-brain developed the ability to under-stand relationships in space and time. The left-brain became responsible for fine physical manipulations, and language. Whatever is the genesis…literacy, language, and any of its associated symbolic representations, is here to stay. These human powers are mostly a blessing, but sometimes they are misapplied.

Symbolic representation such as language, which has the ability to be communicated *across more than one physical sense*, is a quality possessed by the human race alone. Dogs and dolphins lack the alphabet or Braille, or a national constitution. We seem to be the only ones privileged to transmit language using multiple mediums. We transmit symbols through speech, through sight and through touch. Language that is transmitted across the senses, and on this scale, is absent in any other species, perhaps even in the entire cosmos. There is no proof to this date otherwise. As of now, we are probably the sole literates of the Universe.

> Symbolic representation such as language, which has the ability to be communicated across more than one physical sense, is a quality possessed by the human race alone.

Nevertheless, consider that this information age affects the literate and educated more damagingly than the less read. We, the literate, encounter volumes of information. This information can be constructive as well as destructive. Words are only a tool, and therefore people can use them for both good and bad. Tomes such as national constitutions, and Hitler's, *Mein Kampf,* are all part of this collection of information. Different versions, new facts, and news are constantly pounding the literate.

A metropolis would have many newspapers. An adult literate person like Nachiket would probably have read works of several authors. Different media expose the individual to various ideologies. There are views on reality and ideas in worlds of fiction that influence our thinking. We have ideas that contradict other ideas, as also ideas that seem correct, but turn out to be incorrect later. Ideas in politics, the sciences, humanities and the arts keep changing. One may have accepted a lot of information from different sources as plausible simply because there are no alternative explanations.

When scientists declare that life-forms seen today are the result of 'natural selection[5]' or when economists say that the market is driven by 'competition[6],' or when gurus proclaim that 'self-enlightenment[7]' is our most important goal—people accept these as true. We could also have accepted without question some 'facts' handed down by family and friends. To help cope while growing up, many of us absorb half-truths and justifications. This could range from distorted religion to homespun wisdom. When we need help, we read books or listen to proclaimed masters of ideologies. Often, this information is incomplete, and susceptible to challenge as we mature.

Some of us keep questioning our situation. We continue to ask 'Why me?' or 'Why this?' every now

---

[5]    Charles Darwin—On the Origin of Species (Nov 1859)

[6]    Adam Smith—The Wealth of Nations (1775)

[7]    Self-enlightenment is a core concept of the Hindu religion, as also a Buddhist belief.

and then, despite umpteen attempts to explain and rationalise all that we face. As thinking beings, we seek complete explanations. We like to believe that what we sense in our reality is wholly true and can be validated. Quite a few of us miss the fine print that our lives may never be verifiably complete, wholly truthful or always just. For example, theoretical economics suggests that the markets can ensure the best succeed using supply and demand as tools to sift through mediocrity, and give merit just recognition. In fact, society may fail to reward merit in many cases. We already know from news or experience that the norms of truth and justice are sometimes transgressed by society.

Our predecessors have handed down a whole bunch of assorted theories, some of it, perhaps as old as the advent of language itself. Despite its age, most of our theoretical knowledge has evolved in isolated pockets of understanding. This is because of geographical remoteness between early human settlements, language barriers and the continuing tendency of knowledge streams to specialise. Theory also seems inadequate because of practical limits in expression using any language. No existing ideology, including the idea that merit is rewarded, seems complete in itself. This is why several ideologies— leftovers from yesterday—are in conflict today. The fact that religions continue to engage in one-upmanship is testimony to the confusion caused by the written word. No ideology, it appears, can offer convincing explanations in isolation.

Conflicts continue, as the world gets smaller and smaller, as the sciences, technology and dominant societies advance, breaching boundaries. When early tribal communes came upon confusing cultures, they pillaged and burned. This goes on even today, but with new tools, and through new methods. The traumatic events in the history of humankind caused by conflict in fundamental thought have left—and continue to leave—deep scars on the human social psyche.

Our being literate exposes us to several conflicting theories, contradictions and variations, some within specific streams of thought. Our fictional Nachiket accepted theories from books and bystanders before waking up to the conflicts and inadequacies in them. We may have mechanically imbibed some flawed theories too. We may have accepted many popular theories as they help us conform.

The primary impact from these popular theories is in our accepting, without question, the purported benefits of competing and winning. There are significant psychosocial pressures seeded in us by popular thought; this includes a pressure to *succeed* at any cost, and baseless fears instilled in us regarding our condition tomorrow. These typically prompt us to worry, compete and overcompensate on everything today for a supposedly better tomorrow. This may be angst of no enduring usefulness, as we shall see going forward.

People, without proper preventive and corrective information, are susceptible to psychological damage, some of which may manifest as symptoms of mental illness. We are in dire need of

> We are in dire need of information that can help each of us design our individual solutions.

information that can help each of us design our individual solutions. We need our own, practical and complete worldview, which is unique and personal, yet compatible with others. People will have conflict and be confused if they stick to book-learning or popular thought, instead of forming a broad, yet personal and practical worldview.

New understanding on human conflict and flawed learning can help us put together this personal independent worldview, and enhance our *sense* of success. Many psychosocial compulsions in our collective learning, elaborated on further in the forthcoming sections, are so forceful that we need a new approach to reach the common psyche enveloped in faulty learning. The approach could be as mundane as techniques that help in being confident or proactive, or, as philosophical as the *meaning of life.*

### *Section Highlights:*

- The human race could be the only species in existence possessing the trait of advanced symbolism and language.
- Our theoretical repository is often confusing and contradictory because theory is an inadequate tool to capture the practical accurately.
- The literate tend to imbibe conflicting theories before they get to form their own unique worldview (by which time, the damage may already have been done).
- The prime theoretical belief handed down and accepted popularly is the need to compete, win and be one-up on others.

- The need to compete, win and be one-up on others may be a flawed consequence of both natural selection, and that of the collective nurture by society.

- Our social structures ostensibly uphold parity, fair opportunity and recognition of merit, but, many norms seem actually biased towards preserving the status quo, good or bad.

- Having explanations for why and how we are conditioned by collective influences can prevent us from slipping into (or help in recovering from) damaging thought.

## ECLECTIC ESPERANTO

Many individuals with schizophrenia observe their surroundings with a heightened sense for detail. They could experience olfactory or auditory hallucinations. Such hallucinations override any comfort the person could have had with his situation, prior to the disability's onset. The person possibly never felt a need to question his worldview, up until the experience of schizophrenic symptoms. Often, afflicted individuals, caught in the novelty of the experience, imaginatively construct inter-connected patterns, arrangements or groupings. They may build delusions using these spurious connections. It is a desperate attempt to impart structure to their reality, which may appear to them as dissolving into chaos. The inter-connectedness imparted may be as simple as reading coincidental relevance in a stranger's passing statement with one's own thoughts. Alternatively, it could be as complex as reading peculiar meaning or even hostility, in physical arrangements in the vicinity.

We can extrapolate from Marshall McLuhan's insight that schizophrenia may be a consequence of literacy, and extend this species-centric ability of literacy to be the basis for some oddities in perception. We can suggest that our being literate prompts us to look for a flawed kind of meta-meaning, beyond the stated or the obvious. Discerning this kind of underlying meta-meaning is perhaps similar to an individual guessing the story of a comic book based only on its illustrations. The conclusions reached by the individual are mostly different from the intent of the writing in it.

Individuals with schizophrenia may seek to validate this kind of meta-meaning. These individuals may have paranoid delusions that others are trying to trick them. Many people with the malady see a huge knotted-up spaghetti-like conspiracy in their situation. The person typically identifies himself, the spouse, a neighbour, the government, a foreign power, or sometimes, a fictional being, as the primary player in such conspiracies. They may feel others know something, which they do not. They may feel others are using esoteric knowledge to undermine them.

Many afflicted individuals probably lacked the knowledge, which could have helped them avoid sinking deeper into the condition. Granted, there are reams written

Many afflicted individuals probably lacked the knowledge, which could have helped them avoid sinking deeper into the condition.

on schizophrenia, but nothing comes close to explaining the strange meaning many with the condition experience. Actually, there probably is no formal theory, which has admitted the existence of, leave alone attempted explanations for, such strange patterns and unusual classifications. Nachiket saw a strange patterning and connectivity, and spiralled into a delusion that God had granted him special powers. He created the mythological Nachiketa as a superhuman alter-ego, because of the out-of-the-ordinary experiences he had at the onset of his condition.

*** 

Can we put forth a hypothesis, taking a cue from schizophrenia, that bizarre inferences and connectivity exist, and are experienced by 'normal' people too? Is there really an underlying order and meaning for us to infer, which is not just imaginary? Can we propose there is a possibility that people demonstrate an odd symbolism as a result of past impressions in our physiology? We are unsure, using current science, if language and the perception of patterns actually reside in our physiology as a species. Our genes may only facilitate our capacity for language by enabling body infrastructure like the advanced human voice box. Nevertheless, consider for now a possibility that some symbolism is embedded in our physiology. An American linguist, Noam Chomsky, has put forth similar hypotheses.

Noam Chomsky proposed Nature might pre-wire our bodies for language. He suggested people possess an innate 'language acquisition device' (LAD). This LAD may express itself as a pre-existing symbolism, common to us all. People demonstrate such symbolism without any external tutoring. Chomsky apparently gave up the LAD in favour of a 'principles and parameters' approach. According to this new framework, some principles and parameters are part of a genetically innate universal grammar (UG). This genetic grammar, he claimed, exists in all humans. Regardless of whether it is the LAD, UG, or something else, there does seem to be some strange underlying symbolism and patterning, an inferred meta-meaning, which is specific to our species[8].

There could then be two possible biases in our foundational and symbolic learning. They are our 'individual' learning, and a larger 'collective' learning as a species. People learn

> People learn symbolism and pattern-recognition as individuals in their lifetime, and perhaps, we learn as a species as well, over eternity.

symbolism and pattern-recognition as individuals in their lifetime, and perhaps, we learn as a species as well, over eternity. A distinct package of shared learning could be resident in some common repository for us. For the sake of identifying this repository in our discussions, we shall call it the *collective mnemonic* (See figure Pic. 1). The collective mnemonic is a collection of influences that we subscribe to, often unconsciously, prior to our becoming aware of our ability to be proactive.

---

[8] Note—the interpretations of corporal and other symbolism presented as we go ahead are the author's own extension of Chomsky's work, with no intention of undermining or distorting his original analyses.

Pic 1. Depicting the construction of the Collective Mnemonic

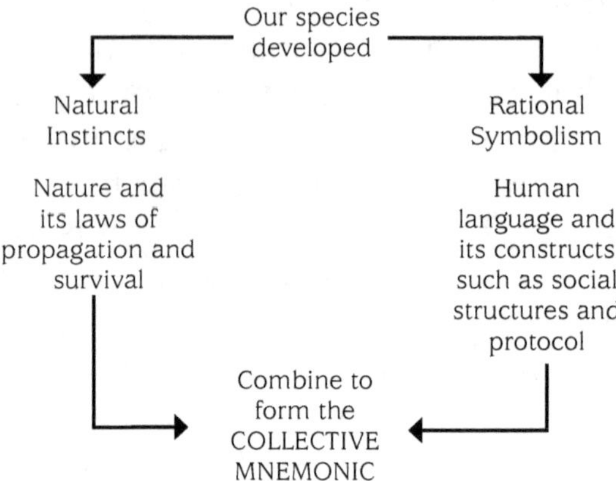


This learning then, which we *assimilated* as a species and as individuals, could induce strange perceptions. It often manifests as a sensing of peculiar cues from the surroundings. Some of the more sensitive people become aware of a subtle symbolic connectivity and cues. They sometimes become uncomfortably conscious of the details in their surroundings and even display odd symptoms as per our current interpretations of mental health. But then, normal people too seem to sense the cues and psychosocial pressures. This allows us to posit the existence of an overlaid common language; a language that defies a uniform classification nonetheless.

People sense cues of the hypothesised collective mnemonic as unusual gestures, inordinate labelling, overlaid associations, and uncommon meanings in what is otherwise trivia. Consider them as a perception on a plane similar to the unspoken chemistry that exists between people. This 'chemistry' gives people the ability to sense fatigue or confusion, or read the body language of others, based on subtle cues. Several would agree, from personal experience, that such cues and unexplained connectivity do exist, but many are also unaware. A good number are ignorant of such under-lying psychosocial pressures and cues of the collective mnemonic, sometimes for all of their life, as they are 'walled-in' solidly by theory.

Some sufferers overlay surreal meaning to the cues, because they want to vindicate the new kind of sensing or awareness that they have suddenly come to experience. For example, they could encounter social labels classifying individuals into predominant personality types such as *usual, real* and *natural*. People, in certain cultures mention such labels, often as subliminal asides, when in conversation. Such labelling seems to slot people into different demeanours. A strange taxonomy labels a person who is functioning predominantly by instincts as a *natural*, a person with complete lack of psychic beliefs or connectedness as *real,* and persons exhibiting typical or typified behaviour as *usual*. When one senses such labelling for the first time, the person could feel diffident or taken aback.

Another example of an oddity that could disturb some people is a sharp intake of breath by another when criticisms or judgements are passed. Stressed persons get uneasy, as they read the sucking action negatively—for example, as siphoning away drive or motivation! Alternatively, this sucking action is sometimes interpreted as acknowledging an expressed appreciation. A good many ostensibly sane people also find a strange double-speak in some utterances—for example, the response 'Fine!' could seem somewhat non-committal instead of affirmative. Furthermore, the mind has a peculiar tendency to derive meaning frivolously and imaginatively from phonetic associations. It sometimes ascribes an alternative meaning based on the phonetics of the word or words. For example, 'window' could be associated with winning money or *win dough* (as, tongue-in-cheek, Microsoft would readily testify!). But, these inferences are not always playful or entertaining and can sometimes be disturbing. Such inferences, often nonsensical, follow from the afflicted mind's inclination to relate everything in the environment to the person's primary concerns.

Potential schizophrenia victims are generally introverts, and initially, remain unaware of the collective biases and cues around them. Some begin sensing the bias and cues for the first time, only at the onset of the psychotic condition. In many cases, they cannot distinguish practical and valid social responses or cues, from the flawed or nonsensical ones. Aspects in these cues that can help are typically missed and bundled up with the ones that can harm instead. Some cues, such as those contributing to insight, can be valid as devices in social interaction. However, the flawed ones, such as those prompting us to hurt ourselves or *conquer* others, may harm us.

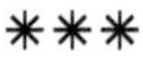

Dr Dharmaraj, our maverick psychiatrist, suggests there are 'subtle' and 'gross' cues in the collective mnemonic. Some oddities lend credibility to the existence of such cues and the collective mnemonic. For instance, sensitive individuals may notice a subtle body language in toddlers. A sensitive person may feel that toddlers communicate using bodily postures even before they learn a language! An example is when the person attributes meaning to toddlers patting their right thigh reflexively during an adult discussion. Some interpret this action as an indication that the discussion is heading correctly. They feel cued-in despite the discussion being complex and beyond the comprehension of the toddler displaying the gesture. We could have also observed instinctive gestures and postures in adults, playing to the state of mind or the situation. Examples are, unconscious tendencies to crack one's knuckles to indicate agreement, and rub one's palms together to indicate starting afresh. These are bodily responses to arrangements in the vicinity and lack universally deducible explanations. They reflect an obscure symbolism[9].

Some people read cues from the collective mnemonic as signs meant to communicate. Some see them as mystical prompts. Many others, as said earlier, may remain ignorant that they even exist. Such manifestations, when sensed for the first time, could cause feelings of confusion, inadequacy and fear. They can block out the rational mind, or, at the very least, impede its ability. The peculiar meaning bestowed on the ordinary and inane is analogous to the interpretation of body language. Our explanations are inaccurate at times. Who is to say a posture is natural or intentional? We can merely conclude that there is an attempt to communicate. Like body language, several

---

[9]    More examples of such connectivity as a result of the collective mnemonic are provided in Chapter 5, In-Sanity.

of the cues are coloured by personal interpretations, although there are some collectively accepted hunches for many of them. Cues from the collective mnemonic are like *Esperanto* in that it is common to many as a mode of communication. Yet, it is eclectic enough to prevent being systematically organised.

Even if Nature does not pre-wire us symbolically as a species, we could acquire specific instincts in regards to symbolism early on in our lives. History is not new for every baby born. This Creation and civilisation are not new worlds for every new birth. Hence, we acquire symbolic learning right from our birth, through social interaction. It is likely that every age provides some tutored symbolism as instincts, which are specific to that point in time. The sum of information developed until that age 'indoctrinated' the child born in the times of the Roman Empire or the Victorian era. Our environment too houses an external storehouse of centuries of civilised thought and practices. This storehouse drives an early subtle conditioning in us with regard to aspects such as competing, winning, contorted labelling, patterning, etc. It also inculcates questionable practices and outdated beliefs of a more obvious and gross nature.

Examples of that which is gross in the collective mnemonic are plentiful. They abound in religious and traditional practices. One example of a social influence from the past is the Hindu practice of isolating menstruating women. The Hindu scriptures claim the presence of such women desecrates religious rituals.

Some Hindu women today, take modern medicines to postpone their periods, and avoid any possible clash with a planned religious ritual. Christianity and other religions also have their share of obscure beliefs and practices. When people go through their rituals, mumbling some archaic words, perhaps in Latin, many wonder if everything went right. Explanations given by priests are usually inadequate, and often based on unsupported symbolic associations. While we seem to be getting civilised in many aspects with time, certain traditional practices carried into this age may be pointless, and sometimes damaging as well.

✳✳✳

Instincts and impulses that manifest from our core are likely to be pure, as captured in some art. However, a flawed and incomplete symbolic learning, assimilated over generations, seems to have corrupted a large portion of the collective 'civilised' memory. If we go by subtle or gross cues from the collective mnemonic, we may hit paradoxes or contradictions. In its mildest form, the inability to respond to such roadblocks in thinking could cause a little anxiety or slightly irregular behaviour. In a severe form, this could contribute to full-blown schizophrenia with its delusions, hostility and other symptoms.

Some of the cues and manifestations, one may hazard on the positive side, should be seen as metaphorical expressions presented by the collective mnemonic to set right deep-set trauma. The trauma, as suggested earlier, may range from innately painful birthing experiences as a species, to unresolved impressions of abuse in individuals. This is experienced differently by each individual. This kind of individual differentiation is yet another reason why the collective mnemonic defies being categorised easily.

Therefore, in addition to the first problem of 'flawed theory,' which presses us to compete and win, there is a close second in collective cues. Since some see common manifestations

> Our symbolic reality seems arranged in a bizarre and surreal kind of order, unlike any described in books.

and similarity in meanings to the otherwise *'illiterate'* social cues, we can guardedly conclude there *is* a different hidden order around us. We can tentatively conclude that social indoctrination and cues, both subtle and gross, exist in our core collective instincts or mnemonic. Our symbolic reality seems arranged in a bizarre and surreal kind of order, unlike any described in books. This is the second problem that leads to unhelpful thinking.

These underlying biases and cues could be particularly frustrating for the literate when stumbled upon, because they challenge the boundaries of theoretical learning. When we sense such cues for the first time, they might be shocking. For a person with schizophrenia, the cues may be hostile. We are going to explore these ideas and provide suggestions, which should help many of us acquire a sense of control and poise. We can close many gaps between what we see in our reality and what we know about it.

<u>*Section Highlights:*</u>

- We, the human species, have absorbed some symbolism as part of our physiology or mental make-up as we evolved.
- This absorbed learning is in our collective memory. It causes some people to read symbolic cues in their environment.
- The book refers to this collective memory as the *collective mnemonic*. This manifests as body language, social labelling, irrational traditional beliefs or mysticism, and some absurd, yet provocative, symbolic associations.
- If we sense such cues, they may influence our decisions, as they suggest a meaning of a different order. Some people appear to know this order while some others cannot fathom it.
- When those who go largely by theory become aware of such cues, the cues can be confusing, or appear to have a mystical basis.

**2**

# WITHIN

'Come in, Nachiket,' the doctor said, and gestured for him to sit. 'I read what you have written. It is quite interesting!'

'Tell me, am I right?' Nachiket inquired, taking a seat.

'We shall see as we go on,' the doctor said in a disarming manner. 'How are you feeling?'

Nachiket got into the discussion straightaway. 'There is still a crowding of thoughts. You had asked me if I was awake or asleep. The question really intrigued me as I relate it to personal awareness. How do people become aware well in time? Doesn't the delayed realisation of my ability to be proactive put me at a disadvantage? Where is the justice, O Lord of Dharma, for I do not choose every situation in which I find myself?'

The doctor forced himself once more into the role, wondering where this was going. 'A drive to wilfully improve our situation is a result of us becoming aware.

Until such an awakening, you had no need to question your situation or weigh your actions. You were kind of floating without a rudder. You may have been diffident or aggressive, and acting impulsively. You keep reacting because several of the social measurements you have accepted, force you to think you are in an advantageous or a disadvantaged position. Such social measures and judgements, which we subscribe to are also a part of an involuntary learning we imbibe, much before we become aware of ourselves and our unique capabilities.'

Nachiket was indignant. 'The dice seem to be loaded. Those who have been aware long before me could downplay or impede my efforts at progress.'

'Perhaps, but consider that many of these forces are the result of years of social evolution,' the doctor said in a placatory tone. 'Many social devices try to provide us with a protected waiting place before we can go where each of us choose. This waiting place could be bare, or luxurious—mentally, menially or materially. You must accept whatever it is currently and aim at progress. If you do not accept and aim to improve, you may stagnate or be filled with damaging thoughts.'

'So do society's declarations of what is progress, what is right and wrong, and what is desirable cause these aberrations?' questioned Nachiket, pushing to zero-in the blame.

'Not quite,' countered Dharmaraj slowly. 'As an advanced species, you did not get where you are without also gathering a set of rules provided by Nature. Long before language became a given, the rules humankind lived by were akin to those of animals. This was the way the cosmos cradled you. Such laws are also residual in you, and they may influence the way you react.'

'Therefore, it's a double whammy! Both nature and nurture force me to be abnormal before I can take control consciously,' said Nachiket. He was still looking for something to blame.

Dharmaraj smiled in a conciliatory manner and continued. 'This is why we, the thinking and feeling human beings, seem to have developed a tool to acquire and store knowledge—spoken and written language. As a human being, this tool is your birthright.'

'What about the rest of nature? Are other beings handicapped?' asked Nachiket.

'Perhaps the venue for the human being to apply such a tool is now evident. In you are, both, an illiterate instinct and a literate guide. The human being, at the pinnacle of the evolutionary pyramid, has a duty to himself and society, and a responsibility to care for Nature. There are several roles for a human being to play and several goals—personal, social and natural. A portion of popular understanding proclaims some goals as superior. However, one destination is not superior to any other. How you choose to follow progressive social and natural directives determines your future,' said the good doctor, putting the ball back in Nachiket's court.

'How can that be?' asked Nachiket. 'Are you saying my choices, rather than civilisation's assessments, determine what I should do and what is success? That my choices are as valid as the norms of civilisation?'

'Not entirely,' said Dharmaraj. 'I merely say the choice that you wholly own is the best choice. Civilisation may measure success as a mix of mental, material, spiritual, or physical objectives. Alternatively, it could be palpable only to you as your own measure of success. Civilisation can tailor your choice, which is usually a relative measure, or you can make a more enduring independent choice. You will not have internal confusion if you own your choices, social and personal, and accept the consequences.'

'...and before I learn to choose, the choices of others control me?' Nachiket concluded meditatively.

Dharmaraj smiled. 'There is a Zen saying, "When the student is ready, the teacher appears." Until you become aware of your ability to choose, you are just not ready.'

'How can existence accommodate the choices of everybody? Are we to be eternally in conflict? Is this conflict not negative?' Nachiket queried.

'We will take this up later,' said the doctor, winding up the session. 'Answer me carefully: Do you see, hear or smell things that don't seem to have an explicit source?'

'Sometimes,' Nachiket answered. 'Mostly, I hear nothing other than your guiding voice, Lord.'

'Are you sleeping well?' the doctor sighed and inquired.

'Yes, a little,' Nachiket said, 'but it is like an intoxicated state. I am neither awake nor asleep.'

'I am writing down some more pills you have to take,' the doctor said. 'Let me assure you things will get clearer as we progress.'

Nachiket's parents told the doctor that Nachiket seemed calmer. He had begun eating and sleeping a little. The doctor prescribed a very mild sedative to help Nachiket when he had difficulty sleeping. He suggested keeping a simple routine for Nachiket at home. The doctor also warned the parents that recovery may be slow. The family needed to be patient.

# A PRIMAL PERSUASION

When one observes the peaks and valleys of sanity that we display as a race, one wonders, *Are we civilised?* Despite phenomenal advancements in technology and means of communication, the collective human psyche of today still has flaws. What we know of the gradual development of civilisation is fraught with barbarism, some of which continues into this age. People snuffed out human life without as much thought as they would give to killing an insect, and, many still do. Inhuman behaviour continues to occur in this advanced age. Most of us are able to appreciate the 'sensible' around us, although horrible news and happenings seem ubiquitous. We, quite mechanically, distance ourselves from obvious cruelty or plain evil to retain our sanity. When we hear of atrocities such as police torture or rape, we note them and can, and perhaps should, respond with displeasure. However, if we *obsess* over them manically, it can be disturbing. If negativity bombards us without any limits, filtering or safe rationalisation, it would be impossible to keep sane. The underlying cause of schizophrenia may be a perception of an overwhelming negative environment.

> If negativity bombards us without any limits, filtering or safe rationalisation, it would be impossible to keep sane.

Though society does provide several dos and don'ts, it appears we have been unable to inculcate universal humane values successfully. The continuing brutality suggests there *are* flaws in humankind's primal learning, social instincts, and knowledge base. Schizophrenia may arise from an inability to filter out or rationalise negativity and aggression in a safe manner. An afflicted person may read meaning into harmless occurrences. For instance, a person with schizophrenia might be shaken by the action of somebody aggressively drawing a chair closer. The afflicted person may not have come across or read of such an invasion of private space before, and builds on it negatively to the extreme. It could cause an afflicted individual to become diffident and closed, or prompt hostility. The patient could see it as part of a full-blown delusional conspiracy. The condition usually precludes any rational response by the patient, such as asking the instigator the reason for the invasive action.

The two problems of flawed theory promoting competing and winning, and, that of 'illiterate' cues from the collective mnemonic could interact. Are basal, illiterate and natural instincts influencing civilised thought? For example, the Darwinian theory of Natural Selection is sometimes (even 'popularly') misunderstood. The principle of 'survival of the fittest' is sometimes skewed and applied in the social context instead of restricting it to the Natural. Norms that promote individuals or groups to be one-up on others are widely touted and unthinkingly accepted.

> Norms that promote individuals or groups to be one-up on others are widely touted and unthinkingly accepted.

True civilisation can flourish only with cross-cultural celebration and etiquette. However, several people tend to sacrifice this etiquette. They consider success as being victorious over others. But, for a person to merit the term civilised, celebrating any and all constructive beliefs in the social, economic, and political spheres is required, not victory over them. Some may be blinded instead, by their own understanding and conclude others are inferior. The basis for Nazism and the doctrine of Aryan superiority came from a refusal to accept any other understanding.

Humankind has filled literature that leans towards romanticism with what *should* be (mostly positives), while, its classical renditions seldom candidly reflect what *is* (which can be barbaric). We need our heroes and happy-endings. This is the way literature has always been and probably always will be. Much of our 'developmental' literature also focuses on our degree of *relative* success. Moreover, today's media is inclined towards highlighting such successes. Some objects and the social status they bestow seem more desirable than others are. We are flooded with information that makes us question the adequacy of our lifestyle and contributions.

> We are flooded with information that makes us question the adequacy of our lifestyle and contributions.

Most of our sources for information and advice compare people on the basis of ability, power and wealth. They promote the social value placed on superiority. Many have acquired twisted and unhelpful instincts because of such misguiding information. In my opinion, people generally are normal thinkers until life suggests they have material, mental, physical or perhaps social inadequacies in relation to others. Some comparisons can make the individual reactive, downhearted or discouraged.

The corruption of the pure and gentle instincts of the human species could be a historical fact. In this seems to be the genesis and continuity of discontent and confusion in society. People simply deny their situation and respond to the environment with suspicion, aggression and cynicism. Or conversely, they can choose to learn proactively and become confident, however devastating or unstable the circumstances seem to be.

***

How did an aggressive philosophy promoting conflict begin? Why do some people deem it necessary? I put forth the following hypothesis; my attempt at explaining the origin of misplaced desires, and consequently, that of comparative evaluation. This hypothesis covers the origin of personal desires to become what someone else is, or possess what someone else has. It is an attempt to explain the genesis of the disposition that causes us to compare ourselves with others. This explanation may be applicable to both beginnings of such comparisons in us as a fledgling species, and, its beginnings in children.

Consider, there may have been crossbreeding among early humans with discrete evolutionary paths. That is, tribes separated by great distances for centuries, cohabited with each other when they eventually met. This could have contributed to the availability of larger gene pools. Larger gene pools meant the potential for more advanced brain structures. Some offspring of such unions could therefore have had the potential to be better performers. A unique habitat could also have nurtured special survival skills in some. These two aspects: the union of independent evolutionary paths, and, exposure to different learning environments could have led to novel acts by a few. Of course, in present times, it is exposure and consequent insights, not the gene pool, which lead to most differences in understanding and ability.

The novelty observed in a 'peer' by both the early Neanderthal of the past, and the very young child of today, could trigger two choices: Imitate and learn the observed novel acts if inspired (or required), or, ask a frustrating instinctive question—*How did he do this when I cannot?* This forms the seed of an abstract *virtual scorecard*. This virtual scorecard is largely the basis for all major conflicts amongst people. The scorecard adds various headings such as the extent of understanding, possessions, wealth, power, etc.

The collective mnemonic causes such a scorecard to take shape very early in us. Instead of having a sense of comfort with ourselves we compare ourselves with others, and see relative judgments in everybody else's interactions. Our perceptions of inequity, apparent inferiority or of relative superiority are sometimes misplaced. Our sense of insufficiency *in comparison to others* could be the cause of much conflict. We seek to measure up, almost intuitively, to a comparative standard.

We seek to measure up, almost intuitively, to a comparative standard.

Many people subscribe to comparative standards of worth for their sense of success. For many of us, such a scorecard may be active before speech. The scorecard may have replaced natural and helpful, albeit childlike traits, such as curiosity and frankness with impeding drives like fear and envy. One could try intensely to get good feedback from others using comparative yardsticks, or, build an artificial defence—refusing inputs. Both are extremes when what is required is a balance.

The third problem for us, I feel, is this *virtual scorecard* prompting us to desire what someone else is or has. The scorecard, once accepted, increases in complexity as we live. It has the potential to affect all of us. The aggressiveness that persists in us may not be from our savage beginnings alone. The wildness also stems from a tacit social acceptance of such a virtual scorecard. People susceptible to schizophrenia tend to be sensitive and often feel the scorecard is unjust, whether such feelings are valid or not. Such a feeling was behind Nachiket's persistent one-track questioning and attempts at blaming his environment. Nachiket sensed this social pressure and felt the way out was to question some social norms.

✳✳✳

Patients with schizophrenia may be delusional and extend this problem of comparative measures beyond their own controllable surroundings. They could imaginatively attribute it to a larger conflict, which is typically beyond their ability to influence. For example, they may feel they are in the middle of a tussle between God and devil, foreign powers and country, elitists and the common-man, etc. Many could assume such mega-tussles are part of their primary responsibilities, and attempt ineffectively, to influence them. As a result, some become aggressive or hostile, or sometimes just succumb to an unexplainable confusion.

Normal people too may react atypically when coming out of their theoretical shell. Some feel inadequate when faced with a practical reality. Several make compromises, leading to more and more conflict or confusion. Many feel fear, envy, hostility, self-pity and other unhelpful emotions. All this, merely because what one knows, seems insufficient to deal with what one faces. Does this mean the gap between the practical and theoretical has to continue? No! Not if we add appropriate elements to ideas such as truth, justice, equality, evolution and the like.

We can prevent, or possibly reverse, perceived disturbances in the environment and ourselves. On the one hand, there is aggressive and savage behaviour, and on the other, useful and caring instincts, both in Nature, and society's nurture. How can we manage these two sides or persuasions of Nature and society? Are we learning a useful symbolism intuitively as a species, but with wild Nature, and a social bias to be one up distorting this learning? I propose some new ideas that can help us resolve such distortions. We can align our individual, community and natural directions successfully.

*** *

While Nature seems random and lawless, we could accept that its principles are survival, propagation and balance. People, as discussed earlier, tend to regard the survival instinct and evolution as mechanisms to develop the toughest and the best in the species. However, the rules of Darwinian evolution are callous about being progressive. They only ensure adaptability to the environment. Natural 'law' makes do with just what is sufficient to sustain the procreation of the species. Nature, prior to the advent of language, was sans a cultured, intellectual or other *refined* evolutionary purpose. It was and is brutal.

Joel Achenbach, the *Washington Post* columnist, in his book *Why Things Are*, says, 'Animals don't choose their behaviour. Nor do they, over time, gradually learn that one strategy, of behaviour or growth, is better. What happens is more mechanical than that. There is a competition among genes. The "good" genes, in the generic sense of good and bad, may not always win. The winner is just the one that most successfully propagates, survives, and adapts best. Take the example of the genitalia of a drone bee exploding and injecting a virgin queen bee with sperm, while effectively plugging her up from all other drones. We could agree that a gene that causes a bee to explode is a bad gene, yet it is perfectly obvious that the exploding-genitalia gene would win the contest because it literally shuts out the competition. Nature is therefore coldly logical, but extremely stupid in some sense. *Nature rewards behaviours that impede or destroy rivals* (sic)[10].'

In the light of the above, how can we care for Nature and at the same time reap its bounty as early Native-Americans purportedly did? Has society contributed to

---

[10]    Joel Achenbach; Why Things Are: Answers to Every Essential Question in Life; New York: Ballantine Books; 1991

deep flaws in us because of the way it has nurtured us? Do our natural beginnings make humane society impossible? In defence of Nature however, is its other principle: *balance*. We can look at balance in two ways: as an inherent property of matter through 'entropy,' and, in human beings and social systems through the harmonising tool of literacy. Entropy is a scientific principle relating to the field of thermodynamics. This principle states that all physical imbalances in an isolated system, such as temperature and pressure, tend to even out over time.

The doctor suggested that Nachiket consider another dimension of balance in Nature, similar to entropy, which *includes the literate human being*. Balance in Nature, I hazard, is inherent at one basal level—the material—through entropy, and implied at another level through the growing literacy of the human species. From one perspective, Nature is illiterate, and from another, It could have facilitated the development of literacy as a harmonising tool to enable us to look after It. If wild nature suggests aggressive survival, a civilised human nature suggests superior balance.

If wild nature suggests aggressive survival, a civilised human nature suggests superior balance.

Is literacy then a final attempt by Nature to ensure the continuity of this ecosphere? Is literacy part of a primal persuasion, nudging us to be humane and caring? Are people being responsible if this is so? Should we pause and ask ourselves: *Is civilisation set on a self-destruct mode?* It could be a huge problem for us as a collective entity if we continue to use our natural beginnings or material imbalances as an excuse for destructive and corrupt behaviour. We need to use this unique human platform of literacy to convince ourselves and collaborate. Using literacy as a tool, we need to save the environment and our race.

*Section Highlights:*
- The collective mnemonic indoctrinates people, early in their lives, that they have to conform to some discriminatory protocol and certain social expectations.
- The belief that one needs more than others, could be caused by widely prevalent comparative measures and expectations—a *virtual social scorecard.*
- The scorecard engages us in flagrant comparisons without regard for humane values and is insensitive. This can give rise to damaging thoughts, words and deeds.
- The scorecard and our savage illiterate natural beginnings make a *humane* society difficult to conceive and achieve.
- The development of literacy in our species could be part of a bigger Natural plan to disseminate environmental consciousness and ensure social harmony.

## THE FLAWED GESTALT

Much of the deficiencies experienced, feelings of inadequacy, and lack of purpose, I posit, are rooted in the problems cited. These are also the likely candidates contributing to the onset of schizophrenia. At the risk of being repetitive, let's tie up the ideas so far. First, we discussed that flaws in civilisation's theory tend to corrupt learning and knowledge of what we should do or achieve. Several thinkers, in the available theory, appear to promote winning and competing unabashedly as our only worthwhile goals. Our thinkers may have had the right intent, but existing theory is misinterpreted, and fails to define and capture what is enduring accomplishment. This has left a vast majority of the population, who should feel good about what they are, feeling short-changed instead.

Then, we talked of the possibility of an illiterate nature mimicking intelligence and passing on incorrect symbolic cues. People sense these symbolic associations under stress or in psychotic states. The cues may be generic, or conversely, related allegorically to specific personal trauma. We also discussed the faulty standards of success in society, which peddle virtual social scores. Many popular social standards of today condone damaging desires, aggressive posturing, and unreasonable behaviour, as long as these traits conform to the social *game*. Our reward mechanisms often treat these traits as helpful for a person to survive and to achieve *success*. However, as the standards themselves appear to be in constant flux, it seems to me there are low, almost impossible odds for one to feel successful consistently using such measures.

There is more. All of us have gone through trauma in our birth experiences. The changes taking place in our physiology while transitioning from the womb are staggering. Intra-uterine life is very different from life outside the womb. During birth, the umbilical vessel spasms shut. Blood no longer comes from or goes to the placenta. In addition, the following changes take place, sometimes too rapidly, causing shock:

- A hole in the heart closes.
- The lungs now inflate and oxygenate the blood.
- The liver now metabolises.
- The kidneys now filter the blood.
- The GI (gastro-intestinal) tract now absorbs all nutrients.

These adaptive changes must occur in a systematic and orderly manner, and place huge demands upon the new born. The trauma of these sudden changes could cause long-term repercussions. We should understand that such trauma can cause incongruity in some of our early thoughts, words and deeds. Many events happen before we get to realise the right thing to be or do. Some wrongdoings in our life are without any roots in our social or personal decisions, but from unavoidable early trauma. Some of the traumas occur naturally, and some are traumas from abuse. Hence, we must stop blaming ourselves alone and realise there are several contributing factors in the collective mnemonic, good and bad, that have made us who we are today. We can accept, correct, or manage any wrongdoings in our past, and not feel that our guilt or anger is irreparable.

> Many events happen before we get to realise the 'right' thing to be or do.

***

> The collective mnemonic artistically mimics intelligence in a manner that seems to fit-in, but sometimes this is disturbing.

Symbolic cues, introduced in the section *Eclectic Esperanto*, are the most confusing influence to understand among the four problems. This may need elaboration. Just as human artistic expression sometimes goads our dark side; we can propose there is a collective learning in us as a race, which sometimes prompts us to reach disturbing conclusions. The collective mnemonic artistically mimics intelligence in a manner that seems to fit-in, but sometimes this is disturbing.

As discussed, the mnemonic may suggest a meta-meaning in corporal gestures, or by a strange labelling, or phonetic parallelism. It may impart a contorted significance to random stimuli and trivia in the vicinity. In addition, the collective mnemonic could also suggest a different surreal order. It may imply dreamlike coherence and continuity to disconnected events in a waking state. On the positive side, some of the cues from the mnemonic, one may propose, are beneficial. They may suggest ways for the experiencer to either resolve early trauma, or garner a new unique personal learning.

We need not read disturbing meanings into the *artistic language* that Nature presents through the collective mnemonic. Nature does not think. Perhaps someday It will, if our ability to recall our learning as a species exceeds what we can recall as individuals. But then, why would we want it that way? Collective consciousness or intelligence that conflicts with individuality is not in order. I ask—why would anyone want to submit their individuality to what could potentially be mindless collective conformance[11]?

✳✳✳

In closing out Part I, I speculate there is an extremely strong, almost absolute, illiterate Natural force within us. But, there is also a rational impetus driven by literacy in our species. The illiterate Natural force, I believe, is *ignorant* of the nuances of human civilisation and intellectualism. It will pursue what seems 'balanced' within its scope. Nature has the option of excluding an irresponsible species to support its balance. Recent tests on sperm counts of healthy men have indicated a reduction of almost 50 per cent over the last fifty years. Even the quality of the available sperm has declined. This is from research by a Danish paediatric-endocrinologist published in the *British Medical Journal*[12]. Based on this finding, an English author had written a science fiction story in which the last human baby is already born[13]. Is there an evolutionary bias in Nature that is nudging our species out of existence? Has the very same Nature provided us a way to redeem ourselves through the harmonising tool of literacy?

There is no need to get worried, but it does suggest something for us to consider carefully. Some aspects

---

[11] This idea of a collective drive is explored ahead in the section 'Severed Stakes.'

[12] Skakkebaek; Niels E. quoted in, Colborn, Theo et al, Our Stolen Future (1997) Penguin

[13] James, P. D., The Children of Men, New York; Warner Books, 2002

of Nature may be in conflict with an intellectual and cultured humane outlook. The imperfect nurture of human society may be adding to human conflict too. Then again, reason and rationality cannot exist without Nature. But over time, our role as a species has changed from being Nature's dependent wards to being its caretakers. Our need to care for Nature hence has to be part of our social and civic mission. We must care for the environment that originally cared for us. If we become civilised in the true sense, we may still save our species and our only known home in the Universe.

> But over time, our role has changed from being Nature's dependent wards to being its caretakers.

It is hard to consider that these problems exist when you are in the thick of things. We do feel there is a good degree of reason in collective thinking and its norms, and that it is constantly improving. It is comforting to believe our race is rational and mature, and that all natural forces are gentle. But, consider this argument, *the spirit or gestalt of the race could be disturbed.* We know some people continue to regard abrasive instincts such as 'stomp out rivals mercilessly' as normal. These die-hard, unreasonable and opinionated individuals adopt aggressive and destructive drives almost as a habit. They would be sceptical when confronted with the view that humanity *is required* to be humane to qualify as *normal.* We, the living, need to collaborate and course correct as a race... and soon!

So what is the good news? The good news is we *can* manage the flawed persuasions of both nature and nurture. We *can* function effectively with a new set of parameters to evaluate our lives. An imperfect nature and nurture *can* be resolved by internalising new explanations for what we are and what we face. We will realise, soon enough, that we already possess the skills to face and manage creation's *abnormalities*. When our core instincts, our intellect and our interactions get aligned, we would realise a greater altar to dedicate our existence… as a humane, civilised and social being. Such a realisation would enable us to accept ourselves, improve and perform at our best, whether afflicted or normal.

## *Section Highlights:*

- The common human trauma of birthing precedes the three problems of flawed theory, illiterate symbolic cues, and civilisation's virtual scorecard.
- These problems are the bases for inhumane, unreasonable, mystical or superstitious behaviour in otherwise 'civilised' people.
- Unless we, both the afflicted and normal, see reasonable and collaborative living as a must for us as a race, we will have damaging conflicts.
- We can manage any perceived abnormalities by aligning ourselves to a larger plan and purpose.

# PART II: The Preparation

In biology all existing instincts have been grouped into two fundamental classes, according to their ends, namely, instincts for the preservation of the individual and instincts for the preservation of the species. Both cases offer aspects of struggle, connected with transient episodes, and as it were, with encounters between the individual and the environment; and at the same time in both cases there are instincts that show themselves as constant vital guides, with an eminently conservative function... These are the guiding instincts, with which is bound up the very existence of life in its great cosmic function... The guiding instincts therefore have not the impulsive character of episodic struggles, but those of an intelligence, a wisdom, leading creatures on their journey through time (the individuals), and through eternity (the species).

–Maria Montessori, (1870–1952):
*The Secret of Childhood.*

**3**

# CONVERGENCE

Nachiket's parents were eager to know how long it would take him to become normal. Dr Dharmaraj explained there were both psychological and physiological aspects to the problem. He also voiced his concern that Nachiket might need intellectual mentoring as well. He asked the family to avoid discussions on tradition, as the trigger for the problem's onset seemed partly related to unresolved issues relating to it. Nachiket needed to develop his own outlook and discover answers that made sense to him.

Nachiket was in his seat and shooting questions. 'There are times when the next steps are clear, and there are times when it is an effort just to think. A clear head is difficult to maintain. What kind of objective would help us retain our clarity?'

Dr Dharmaraj answered with a question. 'What makes you think a perpetually clear head is a prerogative of the human species? The web of existence binds people and their minds to the physical. We cannot but feel its ramifications. Drop the thought that you must be, or feel 'right,' all the time. Merely accept the consequences of your choices. Whatever be your frame of mind, you will find the motivation to continue acting and better yourself.'

'But the consequences can weigh me down...' Nachiket said.

'Not if you see benefit,' replied Dr Dharmaraj. 'For example, when you see yourself getting up and gaining new understanding, even in a dismal situation, you are walking the path of your chosen evolution.'

'What if my "inner witness" has deep residual impressions from the past that prevent me from walking this path?' Nachiket asked with concern.

Dharmaraj replied, 'It is one thing to say, "I cannot walk," and another to say, "I will not move." You have the programming that prevents you, and the learning that enables you. If the forces that keep you immobile are very strong, the knowledge and rewards on overcoming these forces will be extraordinary. If you get into a state of wanting to move, instead of resigning yourself to immobility, your seed of willingness will sprout. You will find new ways to move, within and outside the boundaries of your residual impressions.'

'If the residual impressions are determined by tradition, culture, and other such things, these may continue to be in our environment. How can we ever overcome these?' Nachiket asked, seeming to get a hint that a fixed stance was incompatible with progress.

'They could be around you, but they would no longer hold their sway when you grant yourself the freedom of choice. New understanding of the same things holding you back is inevitable once you permit yourself to grow. After all, what are tradition, culture, and other forces of civilisation, but the human species in motion over time? When you understand these forces as things you must build upon, you have made them fulfil their purpose as the cradle of your understanding.' Dharmaraj pushed to drive home the point he wanted to make.

Nachiket nodded and said, 'In effect, I could have a problem that is also a tool…'

'Right! Hindu philosophy gave you the notion that people are reborn, but to move ahead, we have to play our current role. This role is not a compromise, but a validation of what we ought to be. If I asked you to consider that you are the Nachiket of this present time, and not someone reborn, how would it make you feel?' The doctor put this question casually, but was tense, gripping the arms of his chair. There could be hostility at his suggestion, but the doctor was guessing the ground was prepared for a positive response.

Nachiket responded quite calmly, 'A little different. What will happen if my current life and my earlier life are in disagreement?'

'They need not be.' Dharmaraj said, relieved that Nachiket's response was not hostile. This meant that Nachiket could yet pull out of his delusion. 'You are a repository of concepts. Once you realise that certain concepts and ideas can be valid for anyone, it is easier to accept them regardless of their source.'

Nachiket continued, remaining unaffected. 'Lord, if the concepts are supreme, then all of us should be subscribing to them. None of us should be disagreeing with another…'

Dharmaraj realised he would have to bide his time for now. He continued explaining, 'The concept is the same, but how we actualise it could be different. A set of abilities and inclinations that are particular to an individual determine the actualisation. It is as if we are all walking different ways to get to our own special destinations. What is common is that we are all moving a step closer.'

Nachiket asked, 'What determines our path and inclinations?'

Dharmaraj introduced the concept of inner intent. 'We have within us an innate natural and rational learning. It is as if there is a spore in us waiting for the right conditions. When our life's purpose aligns with nature and reason, it leads to an easy success. When we lack this kind of purpose, it can lead to conflict within. Our alignment with a clear inner intent will release our true abilities.'

'How do I recognise this in myself?' Nachiket asked anxiously.

The doctor pressed home the advantage, 'When you have completely come to the present and feel each day builds on the previous one, you grow secure in your abilities.'

Nachiket then asked, 'What do I do in the meantime? How do I know I am headed in the right direction?'

Dharmaraj had only one answer. 'Use humanity as a sounding board for your intentions until you can recognise personal benefit in any possible outcome.

This means that faith in the grace of time needs to be a conscious decision. See any conflict as pointing to a course of consistent betterment—the way to an inherent, congruous, but presently impalpable state. See the conflict and confusion as temporary teachers. Act for now with the volition feasible.'

'Then what about spontaneity in action? If I pause to weigh everything, I will not be spontaneous,' Nachiket said, thinking of the times he had acted with no thought for the consequences, secure in his spontaneity.

'The difference is, with healthy instincts you can trust your actions and own the consequences as constructive... although it may not be evident immediately,' the doctor explained.

'What about when others try to force their ideas on me or influence my instincts?' Nachiket worriedly asked.

'Ideas around you are just inputs,' Dr Dharmaraj reassured Nachiket. 'You have to decide what you accept or would like to stand for. We will talk about this sometime.'

Dr Dharmaraj could see the medicine was working, but his interactions with Nachiket were getting intense. The doctor found he had to think rapidly to answer Nachiket's probing questions. The discussions clearly indicated there was a person within, trying to make sense of a confusing plethora of theories and perceptions. The doctor had suggested that Nachiket's delusion was invalid. Anything beyond a suggestion could have triggered hostility. Dr Dharmaraj wondered how much longer he would have to keep up his charade of divinity, and how Nachiket would feel when he ended it.

# THE YELLOW BRICK ROAD

Consider that children are bundles of instinct and reason. If a child's nurturing fails to inculcate responsible behaviour, the child will explore the world of 'bad' instincts. When a ball bounces onto the middle of the road while playing, the child can learn to ask for an adult's help despite a pressing need for the ball. We can teach a two-year-old, with consistent instruction, that to stray onto a road is dangerous. When this knowledge appeals to reason, or gets accepted as the dictates of a higher authority, the child's instinct to run after the ball is checked. Along such lines, the best role instinct can perform for an adult is that of a 'sensing' mechanism. We pass on the sense to our reason to process. If reason validates the instinct, we can act on it. If it does not, we *should* reject it. This then becomes an intelligent proactive choice. Such a choice could seem like a tall order for us, whether normal or afflicted. Nevertheless, we can acquire the skill and wisdom to help us decide when to hitch a ride on our instincts, and when to get off. We can understand when to be detached from instincts, and when to go with the flow. We shall see how.

We often see the making of deliberated choices to be at odds with spontaneity. However, an informed choice is more relevant, and covers a larger context, than an impulsive action[14]. While recognising its value we cannot assume spontaneity is always helpful. We cannot let any flawed conditioning in our past affect

---

[14]  'The terms 'context' or 'contextual' are used in the book to indicate a focus on the real, rational and constructive. Our focus is not mystical, parochial or harmful.

the way we spontaneously and instinctively react today. Instead, it is better to use learning from the past to help weigh decisions rationally and act. Choice backed by experience can become a path *to* spontaneity with greater relevance for the present.

Our instincts emerge from deeper impressions. These are the 'residual impressions' etched in us referred to by Dr Dharmaraj. Some of these impressions trigger instincts that act against personal betterment. They may force the afflicted to stay constrained within the symptoms of schizophrenia. The person may make incorrect decisions, because the instincts in an afflicted person are often flawed. But on the contrary, if we have very well honed and proven instincts, we can arrive at a reasonable decision to trust them. A simple test is to recollect how often you have acted on hunches and been comfortable with the consequences.

No matter how (in) appropriate your instincts are, in abrupt situations, instincts are the primary influencers of action. It becomes vital to nurse back to health any instincts that are in error. We usually regret impulsive actions, but if instincts are aligned with a larger purpose, they do not create regrets. We can realign our stray instincts by acquiring a new perspective. A robust set of instincts would help in focusing actions with their subtle presence. When we nurse these *tendencies* of the mind to be healthy, they aid us in making the right choices.

How do we train and align instincts? We *must first be willing* to move in a progressive direction (the means) despite personal betterment (the ends) being invisible for now. This direction is much like the Yellow Brick Road to the Emerald City in the children's classic,

*The Wizard of Oz.* The principal characters set out on this road to find some things, which they eventually discover, they already have. Dorothy realises she already has the way to get back to Kansas. The Tin Man

> We must first be willing to move in a progressive direction (the means) despite personal betterment (the ends) being invisible for now.

discovers he is not heartless. The cowardly lion finds out he is courageous. The straw-filled scarecrow learns he is brainy anyway. And the wizard, who turns out not to be a wizard actually, only provides each of them a symbolic token of that which they sought, but already unknowingly possessed, as a reward for their quest.

It seems to me, this kind of willingness to believe in something and plough ahead is the way to remedy flawed instincts. This willingness and intent are powerful drivers for energy and success. In it are also the beginnings of personal progress. It feeds the focus and effort that gets results. A half-hearted intent only produces half-hearted acts that fail. The greater the willingness and intent is, the greater will be the effort. Consequently, the quality of decisions, actions, and results is also greater. *The strength of intent might be more important than immediate action.* This is what Dr Dharmaraj was referring to as *wanting* to move. Even if the initial situation is shabby, there is a tendency towards excellence or betterment when there is an appropriate intent. You can always get it right at some point if you have the right intent. With a strong intent, you follow through with appropriate action. We cannot ignite such a powerful intent when our expectations are narrow. However, we would develop a strong enough intent when we get concerned and feel responsible for a broader range of things. Such a broad intent hones our instincts too.

I find we are more likely to deliver value and rejoice in personal evolution if we align our actions with a larger cause or purpose. We need to embed a broader concern in whatever we feel is our personal purpose. We will then see that everyone in this broader range is more than willing to put a shoulder to the wheel. Everyone is involved in our purpose when we are inclusive. Others buy in because they are also a part of the goal. There is great synergy to tap when you commit that a broad range of issues—and not just your personal ones—are going to get better.

We may disagree with others on whether things have to get better, or on how much better they have to get, and sometimes *how* they have to get better. Still, when purpose includes *a concern for a wider range of issues beyond just the immediate self,* such conflicts would get resolved. We will notice all that matters to our progress. We would be able to consider the possibility that all we care about is getting better—in some manner or other. A new sense of clarity will emerge and resolve inner conflict and align our instincts, almost magically. Apparent pitfalls are then seen as only pit stops.

The values of a civilised society are good references for betterment until we realise our personal and independent norms of success. How do we realise such norms? We need to identify and choose our individual purpose, aligned with the process of life. This can happen when we go beyond divisive forces. We can resolve perceived dichotomies, such as those between spirituality and pleasure, between selfishness and altruism, between nature and the intellect, between haves and have-nots, and so on. Such divides get resolved if instead of seeing conflict, we remain constructive and starve the destructive forces. Any inclusive personal purpose would align, I would say almost inevitably, to a human, humane and constructive purpose.

Some people are stuck in questioning the little things when they really should align with a higher purpose. The section that follows provides additional clarity on a set of generalised divisive forces that influence personal purpose. In fact, all that may be required for discovering personal purpose is a catalyst in the form of self-awareness. All of us have it, while it may be dormant in a few. Stay with the big picture that follows and the little things will be irrelevant.

## *Section Highlights:*

- We can align conflicting instincts and reason by having a broader personal intent.
- The intensity of intent ensures our acts are sustainable, result-oriented and excellent.
- We can actualise such a driving personal intent by being willing, open to change and by believing that we do get better… that we progress in some manner or another.
- When personal purpose and intent include larger goals, we experience a bigger synergy and a greater ability for success.

- Recognising such a personal purpose and intent, early on in life, happens rarely because people see dividing walls and divisive forces all around them.

## SEVERED STAKES

Only a few shining exceptions are able to define their purpose early in life. What happens to the rest who seem to be muddling through? Religion and theology provide some tentative rules and abstract explanations on the purpose of life. This keeps several people somewhat content and gives them the patience to wait for concrete 'proof.' Even so, conflicting ideas in religion or ideology are often the trigger for a schizophrenic episode. Harsh as this seems, we should understand that finding logical solutions in religion is near impossible. At best, I suggest that the hopeful amongst us would do better to postpone the attempt until we acquire a sense of readiness. Religious beliefs can collapse under close logical questioning if one is not primed with adequate faith. When we are ready, religion happens—or *unhappens*. Nonetheless, when you already have faith, it is best to keep the faith. It always helps. Religion and faith provide a lot of foundational support that aid the gradual development of personal ideologies, sometimes beyond religious boundaries.

We will explore tradition later as a complete chapter. Meanwhile, here is a peek at an ideological range, without theological overtones. This should help in the recognition of a broader personal purpose. Dr Dharmaraj explained to Nachiket that the power of ideas is objective and independent of individuals. It was part of the effort to woo him out of his delusional persona. The following analysis is an objective concept too, presented with the intent to unite divisive personal drivers.

✳✳✳

There are multi-dimensional forces influencing our mind. To me, three of the obvious dimensions are those of our individuality, community and nature. I have tried to analyse these using a quasi-technical framework, which may not be readily evident to the non-techies among us. We could try capturing a range of ideology along three axes of *individuality*, *community* and *nature* as a 3-dimensional model. The illustration (Table 1): The Axes of Ideology, identifies these 3-D axes with the letters 'I' for the Individual, 'C' for Community, and 'N' for Nature. When a plus sign (+) is placed after the letter, it indicates a constructive outlook along the axis. When a minus sign (−) is placed after the letter, it indicates a destructive or apathetic tendency along the axis. To illustrate, 'C +' means constructive, and 'C −' means destructive or apathetic, along the community axis respectively. The three dimensions of individual, community and nature, along with their two orientations of constructive and destructive, would hence result in eight positions along the 3-dimensional model. That is, combinations of I, C and N, with plus (constructive/ positive) and minus (destructive/ apathetic) signs, result in eight different dominant states. Let us explore what the states represent. This may help in recognising a generic, yet personal purpose.

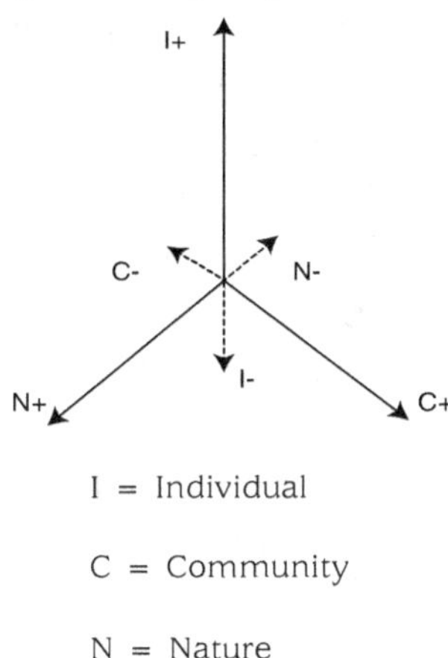


| Sl. | Dimension | Interpretation |
|---|---|---|
| 1. | I – C – N – | Destructive – Sadistic and/or Masochistic |
| 2. | I – C – N + | Primal – No individual or identifiable collective sense |
| 3. | I – C + N – | Orwellian – A dystopian society as portrayed in George Orwell's novel *1984* |
| 4. | I + C – N – | Egoistic – A selfish thinker with no concern for anything other than himself or herself |
| 5. | I – C + N + | Communalist – Such as in an ant society |
| 6. | I + C – N + | An animalistic and territorial recognition of individuality |
| 7. | I + C + N – | Corporate – Nature is assigned a status inferior to personal and collective convenience or comfort |
| 8. | I + C + N + | Personally Purposeful & Reasonable – Humane and constructive |

Table 1. The Axes of Ideology

We begin with the totally negative state along all 3 axes. The 'I – C – N – ' is a completely destructive state, possibly pure evil. The second state, 'I – C – N + ' indicates the condition of a primal entity having no individual or collective goals. It is a life force fuelled by elementary nature. Unicellular life-forms are examples. They fail to show any distinct individual traits or collective behaviour. The Orwellian state (I – C + N –) is based on the author, George Orwell's portrayal of a fictional society. In this, a dictator quashes individual freedoms and natural urges for, what is deemed to be, collective benefit. Such a state proposes the sacrifice of individual and natural drives to serve a supposedly greater collective good. For the egotist (I + C – N –), there is concern for just the self, and no other sense of responsibility. Such a person is callous when it comes to community or nature. In the communalist scenario (I – C + N +) the entity shows no individuality, but is on a kind of auto-pilot mode. This mode, nevertheless, has a group or collective objective. Existence for such entities is along the lines of an ant colony, never questioning natural and collective urges such as foraging for the colony. These entities, as far as we know, may have no sense of individuality, but have enough collective acumen to survive as a species.

An animalistic outlook (I + C – N +) refers to an instinct for survival as a solitary entity or in a pack of their choosing. It usually comes with territorial definitions and boundaries. Such an animalistic entity cannot subscribe to a wider 'civic,' rational or intellectual direction that is inclusive of other beliefs. Next, in the 'Corporate' state (I + C + N –), a tendency to promote convenience sacrifices Nature. This state primarily panders to whatever aids the immediate comfort of the individual and the community. This is often at loggerheads with Nature. It tends, generally, to be ecologically destructive. Several of humanity's pursuits are hedonistic, and with no care for the future of our world as long as we are comfortable today.

> Several of humanity's pursuits are hedonistic and with no care for the future of our world as long as we are comfortable today.

Most personal actions or thoughts lean towards one of these combinations as we confront life. Specifically, instincts for self-preservation, I and N, put up walls against the other influence, of C. Some people see their obligations as part of a civilised race, to be compromising self-preservation. Many see a broad acceptance of different social sub-groups as a threat. A number of social and political factors therefore divide, instead of uniting us. Society seems splintered in its ideologies. The stakes we have, as human beings, seem severed. This makes a personal purpose, which is also universal, hard to realise. It requires including another dimension on the scale of global togetherness, that of C + , without sacrificing self-interest and the well-being of Nature. To don such an all-encompassing position seems difficult, given our dependencies. A personal purpose that has a wider and more inclusive civilised perspective, needs to first be chosen and cultivated.

Dr Dharmaraj was trying to get through to Nachiket that a broad personal purpose includes self-preservation. A negative orientation on even one of the discussed dimensions has damaging repercussions for us. Personal purpose seems elusive, as we are readily able to see diversity; at the same time, we fight shy of picking a position. Acceptance of communal diversity enables harmonious individual living, with a civil attitude of mutual respect and unity. Nobody in this age of interdependence can afford to have a negative attitude towards the global community and Nature. A purposeful direction is one that betters all three facets of individual, nature and community. Such an inclusive purpose, I believe, will ensure our sustenance and survival, both as individuals and as a species.

∗∗∗

How do we choose and invest our efforts when we see several options, with several valid arguments? Actually, I see disagreement as also having a purposeful role. We shall see how personal purpose exists despite disagreement,

> When we align our actions with a broader shared direction, we experience the grace of larger forces, whether we view these forces as divine or mundane.

and, we will see the importance of disagreement itself. A personal purpose includes our need to fight for what we believe to be the best position on the issue. In the chapters that follow, you will see how people can disagree in their beliefs, and yet contribute to betterment. There is more information ahead, which can help unveil a reasonable personal purpose for each of us, despite divisive forces. The information should enable many of us to be productive and proactive, and not victims. The choice, it will be clear, is yours and yours alone. When we align our actions with a broader shared direction, we experience the *grace* of larger forces, whether we view these forces as divine or mundane.

## *Section Highlights:*

- We will find motivation when we subscribe to a wider and more inclusive set of concerns.
- An analysis of individual, natural, and collective drives reveals that being constructive along all three is truly humane.
- Being destructive along any of the three drivers, is the antithesis of humane intent, and invariably precipitates destructive conflict.

- We can recognise a broader driving intent when we come to terms with the legacy of our past, and become open to new learning.

## LEGACY AND LEARNING

As suggested earlier, very few of us are aware early enough in our lives to validate and regulate our assimilation of ideas. Many amongst us have just trusted the environment despite its flaws. This sometimes may have led to harmful experiences. Injuries to a personal cognitive integrity could be a result of internalising flawed and unrealistic schema[15]. This schema includes the cold logic of the 'laws' of Nature, distracting social ideologies, inadequate theory and archaic practices.

I am of the view that far-reaching damages, including personal trauma and abuse, remain unresolved because of an incorrect tutoring by our aggressive age. The impact from such tutoring includes the promotion of flawed social and natural motivators, as well as the teaching of misinterpreted symbolism. I speculate that a mind cannot be a clean slate. The conditioning of the past, may be contorted and burden some of us. Many only build on their flawed past, and never break free. Having an open mind would hence be difficult until our past is resolved, whether we are among the afflicted or normal. Our legacy needs tempering by learning.

*** 

---

[15] Paraphrasing from Stettbacher, Konrad: Making Sense of Suffering: The Healing Confrontation with Your Own Past. New York, N.Y., U.S.A. Meridian, 1993

Dr Dharmaraj pointed out that Nachiket would carry the load of his past until he realised that it involved a great many things outside his control. A legacy influenced Nachiket and his thoughts, words and deeds before he could begin thinking for himself, and weigh the pros and cons. It is so for every one of us. Case in point—we may never be able to address the last of the four problems, our birth trauma. Despite efforts by science to make birthing as free of trauma as feasible, it cannot prevent the shock. This trauma is an explanation for some of the innate *abnormality* we inevitably need to manage. We can let go of everything unhelpful in the times gone by, if we realise that we did not, and cannot always choose with complete awareness.

> We can let go of everything unhelpful in the times gone by, if we realise that we did not, and cannot always choose with complete awareness.

However, not all is dismal. Cognitive learning that is contextual, directs us towards our personal purpose. We seem to have some specific and unique seed awareness that guides us towards betterment. In other words, there is some measure by which an intrinsic core in us is inexorably getting better. Call it wisdom, call it awareness, call it evolution, or call it the path of the soul. There should be no confusion on this basic direction. *Things get better innately in some manner.* When we are ready, we can experience it.

How can we be sure of this? Nachiket felt the ultimate sense of inadequacy when he encountered schizophrenia. We instead, can don an outlook that everything will improve; we can be composed as we wait a while for such an eventuality. We can believe that the purpose of life is growth and recognise that each day builds on the one before. Anyone can discover personal purpose by acknowledging growth. As we go on, Nachiket finally sees that he is where he is, because of all that he had to go through. I myself, continue to live *and seek* my purpose, deficiencies and all, just like the fictional Nachiket. With some belief and commitment, we can learn to celebrate growth, despite experiencing an inadequate present. Growth is certain with a broad canvas for betterment.

> Growth is certain with a broad canvas for betterment.

The first step in recognising one's purpose is to *acknowledge* such a broad canvas for betterment. The art is to recognise, admit and revel in thoughts that confirm the unique progression of our lives. For instance, picturing and revelling in the thought that someone, somewhere, sometime is proud of you. You can celebrate, even before becoming aware of it, the fact that you are getting better; that you are getting proactive; that you are at peace. Expect this.

If things seem hopeless or stagnant at best, we can set our mind to relate to an ever-present personal measure of betterment, in some manner or other. Then, palpable improvement is certain. We are going to see the key principles that make it possible for us to be proactive, for us to understand our uniqueness, and for us to know betterment. We will see how we can readily acknowledge our specific, and constantly progressive, personal purpose.

*** 

The four problems—flawed theory, cues, the scorecard, and early birth trauma—I argue, condition and affect the ways we think, feel and act. As we learn more about ourselves, popular social and traditional diktats could seem discouraging and in conflict with acquiring an independent mindset. For example, we can hit a wall of paradoxes when trying to resolve mystical religious tenets, with what we learnt as progressive or rational in our schooling. Trying to bridge practical reasoning and unusual experiences can lead to distorted conclusions. In some, rigorous attempts at bridging gaps or resolving conflicts trigger mental disabilities such as schizophrenia. Others may go through life with mild to severe unease.

These four problems may be behind a sense of confusion and inadequacy in several people. I believe it is possible to free oneself from the harmful impact of such conflicts. I have been able to apply my new learning to keep schizophrenia in remission, and this learning may be liberating for others too, whether afflicted or normal. Eventually, all the information in the book manifests in three specific life *mantras*. When we are ready, these mantras will seem almost self-evident.

Meanwhile, give yourself the permission to question any destructive power of the past and resolve its flaws. We should eventually get to the point where we can discern order in chaos, see a quantum of success in any outcome, and realise hope in spite of misery. In the next part of the book, in addition to providing more hints on acknowledging personal purpose, we will explore the three addressable problems or 'disorienters' of flawed theory, symbolism and the scorecard (the fourth problem of birthing and infantile trauma can perhaps be managed to a certain extent by resolving the *other* three). We will see how to deal with the primary repercussions of these 'disorienters' in Part III of the book.

## *Section Highlights:*

- Many imbibe flawed social learning and protocol because they are not aware enough, early enough in their lives.
- We cross over to awareness by first acknowledging that some part of us is inexorably getting better, in accordance with an innate personal purpose.
- With growing awareness, we align with such an innate personal purpose.
- A new perspective can rid us of the misleading part of our legacy, and help nurture an awareness of our personal purpose as individuals.

# PART III: The Solution

The demand to be free is the cause of your problems. You want to see yourself as free. The one that is saying 'You are not free' is the same one that is telling you that there is a state of 'freedom' to be pursued. But the pursuit is slavery, the very denial of freedom. I do not know anything about freedom, because I do not know anything about myself, free, enslaved, or otherwise. Freedom and self-knowledge are linked. Since I do not know myself and have no way of seeing myself, except by the knowledge given to me by my culture, the question of wanting to be free does not arise at all. The [preconceived] knowledge you have about freedom denies the very possibility of freedom. When you stop looking at yourself with the knowledge you have, the demand to be free from that self, drops away.

—U.G. Krishnamurthy
(1916–2007) in *Mind is a Myth*

**4**

# EXTERIOR

Dr Dharmaraj knew that Nachiket's path to recovery would require overcoming the positive symptoms (like hallucinations) with medication, and resolving the negative symptoms (like social withdrawal) with fresh thinking. In part, recovery also needed patients to gain enough insight to be able to look at their symptoms with adequate detachment. The doctor was keen to tackle the positive symptoms first, as they were the bigger impediments to recovery.

'How are you, Nachiket? Are the voices continuing?' Dharmaraj smiled and asked, gesturing to a chair.

'Yes. Faintly…like murmurs,' Nachiket replied, settling in. 'However, I hear the voice of a boy from back in my high-school quite clearly. I used to constantly compare myself with him.'

'What does *it* say?' the doctor continued.

'I think he says I am a loser and will never amount to anything in life… It's not very clear…' fumbled Nachiket.

'And what do you feel about this?' said Dharmaraj, in typical psychiatric fashion.

'I feel our discussion will solve this. Winning seems to be everything in life…,' Nachiket stated, letting the words dangle.

Dharmaraj once again picked up the threads, 'Okay, here goes… If winning is everything, then everything must win. This can be a play of words or a reflection of the "win-win" attitude that is at the heart of success. Your earlier questions on conflict of choice have a potential answer. You should check if your choices and their outcome depend purely on *another.*'

'But isn't this true about winning?' Nachiket countered, catching on fast. 'There can only be one clear winner in any game or sport.'

Dharmaraj smiled and said by way of replying, 'A man said, "If your happiness depends on what somebody else does, I guess you do have a problem.[16]" When your focus is not on winning, but on another losing… that is a problem.'

'But how can one win without another losing?' quizzed Nachiket.

'In the game of existence—if you can even call it a game—there are no losers. The secret to winning for oneself is in the continuity of one's confident drive as a player. Humankind has glorified its winners as examples, not because the others should give up and turn away. The problem multiplies because a lot of us

---

[16]	Bach, Richard: *Illusions, The Adventures of A Reluctant Messiah.* New York: Delta, 1998

think those who do not win are losers; that they just fade away into nothing. Rather, the truth is many live equally satisfying lives by choosing to participate in their own independent dimension of success.'

'Are you saying that winning for a cause is also pointless? Why make an effort at all then?' asked Nachiket.

'The hardest thing to give up is a lost cause in which we have emotionally invested,' Dharmaraj responded. 'Actually, no cause is lost. If one could find a way to continue a constructive credo in some other dimension, or in some other form, we remain engaged in a successful pursuit. We need to exercise better choices within the parameters of the possible. It is the stubborn insistence of playing within the bounds originally defined, that may be our undoing. You lose because you have accepted what others have defined as winning.'

'But is it not decided in some way? I do not choose to lose—it just happens,' said Nachiket.

'If you think you have lost… you have well and truly lost,' said Dr Dharmaraj gently, but firmly. 'You can act on the circumstances in which you find yourself. You can open new opportunities. It is impossible to lose, except by your choice to remain in any unpleasant situation that you find yourself.'

'Lord, if you choose to foist a situation upon me, what can a mere mortal do?' Nachiket said submissively, still addressing the doctor as divine.

Dharmaraj sighed unobtrusively at being addressed in this fashion but continued, 'To see the merit in a situation, we need to turn obstacles into stepping stones. One must come out of self-pity and take ownership. When a person is willing to change their circumstances, things that seem magical happen. When we are willing, we notice things that will help us. Then, we are clear, and awake to the chances of turning a situation around. A mortal is not mere, but a bundle of progressive choices waiting to happen.'

'But sometimes the way people want things to happen and the way they actually turn out are different…' said Nachiket, stating a common frustration.

'We don't live in a perfect world. Others, based on their experience, read our actions and reach independent conclusions. If you have provided enough valid options and communicated effectively, the results of your actions will be within expectations. When they are not, you must see it only as requiring yet another action. You cannot control all of your environment's responses, but you have some control over what you can influence.' The doctor based his answer on a version of the Hindu concept, that of a difference between what is fated and what is an outcome of personal action.

'How do I know the difference between what can be influenced and what cannot?' Nachiket asked, still seeming to refuse ownership of his freedom to choose.

'When you create enough options for others to choose from, you are able to influence their decisions,' the doctor said emphatically. 'This requires action and effort.'

'And if the rules for me and around me change?' Nachiket questioned, beginning to realise where the conversation was going, and almost talking to himself.

'You have just answered the question in the question,' the doctor said smiling. 'That is a situation in which you must seek and adopt new definitions of success, a situation where you change too.'

'Can I choose my future, considering what has happened to me in my past life?' asked Nachiket, apparently convinced on the issue.

'Yes!' Dharmaraj exclaimed. 'You can choose a future that is yours and yours alone if you do not compare or confuse it with anyone else's life. For the unique you, it would get better, in some manner or another… if you choose to make it so and appreciate any outcome.'

'But I am afraid. Is there no foundation to my thinking?' Nachiket sounded concerned. 'I feel like I am falling without a safety net. What is happening to me? How long will it take me to adapt?'

'Let's explore this a little more. In our next meeting perhaps… Yes?' the doctor posed gently. 'You will see it is not so much "Why?" or "What?" but that the point is to go forward. You are not alone in feeling fear when facing what seems new. You cannot banish fear, but need to manage it instead. I will teach you some things to do when you are afraid. You will learn and adapt. Perhaps slowly… but, definitely.'

Nachiket felt others were too far ahead for him to catch up. The doctor had discussed seeing one's life as unique instead. Nachiket, to get started, had to learn some coping strategies. He needed techniques that would help him overcome his timidity, and fear of being in what to him was a new environment[17]. The doctor told Nachiket's parents that returning to a normal social

---

[17]   See GLP1 "Flying Above the Flak" at the end of the book under Good Living Practices

life might take a little longer. Nachiket would first need to develop a new outlook that would help him in being confident.

## JONESES SYNDROME

The thoughts that follow would probably be labelled 'leftist' by society's grouping or the social taxonomy. This social taxonomy, I sense, prompts people to label, file and forget anything outside of the existing order. This is a way society protects the status quo. Nachiket, like several of the afflicted, perceived this social labelling and was hell-bent on pointing it out as an injustice. We can transcend much of the labelling and stereotyping, and get a sense of success despite the chaotic packaging and categorisation by the social order. Adopting a new outlook would enable us to be in the 'madding crowd,' and yet, stand apart from its madness.

> Adopting a new outlook would enable us to be in the 'madding crowd,' and yet, stand apart from its madness.

Recall that in the first two parts of the book you got a new take on problems and considered a few unusual thoughts. The purpose behind this sharing was to highlight flaws in collective nature and nurture. This realisation in itself, can point one towards discovering a unique personal purpose. It seems to me that many personal doubts and constraints, which we carry over from the past are, manifest only in part from our own thoughts, words and deeds. Millennia of evolution and several centuries of civilisation have contributed to the glitches in us. As suggested earlier, we could have made choices based on faulty foundational information. We may not have had the ability, early on, to take even an educated gamble. The first two parts pointed out four triggering issues causing flaws in many people. Of these, we cannot completely resolve birth trauma. We, inevitably, need to accept its ramifications and still move on. This Part will address the three other problems that in all likelihood contribute to negative feelings in the 'normal', and lead to mental afflictions such as schizophrenia as well.

Theory and history housed in the postulated collective mnemonic are tricky. Some of history's influences are appropriate while some are not. Appropriate influences guard humane aspects like dignity, individual freedom and self-esteem. But several norms, carried forward into this age by us as a society, clash with these aspects. We saw, earlier in the book, that the collective mnemonic is the source of symbolic cues. Such cues try to maintain the social status quo, and preserve the collective mnemonic's *constricted* definitions of competition and winning. To me, they seem to promote the winning of some at the cost of the others. All loss is glossed over as collateral damage. This aggressive age twists the meaning of victory, to make a virtue of a misguided truth.

The focus of this chapter is hence on what I see as flawed conclusions regarding competition and winning. The chapter highlights society's role in conditioning us to accept the superiority of some popular end-results. Among those that have contributed to these suspect conclusions are our success gurus. Some gurus seem to have done an indiscriminate, and regrettably extensive, selling of competing and winning. Social conditioning and popular belief generally point at the quantum of wealth, or fame or luxury as the true yardsticks of success. Straightaway, such measures deny a sense of success to several contributions, essential to the working of society.

All of us have experienced the simpler manifestations of such core conditioning. It is because of this conditioning, that many feel a compulsion to know, beyond an entertaining interest, who the 'Top Ten Blondes' are, or who made it onto the list of the wealthiest. Such compulsions are ubiquitous and reflect a popular craving for superlative icons. Our social tutoring and rewarding mechanisms compel people to compete for *relative superiority*. The conditioning and cues are so pervasive they would hinder anybody's constructive efforts towards holistic personal wellness.

> Our social tutoring and rewarding mechanisms compel people to compete for relative superiority.

Entire societies, such as the American and Swiss, have ostensibly developed around the principle: *To each his own*. Not a bad idea if it catches on in the true sense. I observe that a majority have forgotten this reasoning and focus too much on winning THE prize because it seems that the winner takes all. Such beliefs create the fanatic; be it a foaming-at-the-mouth greedy business executive, a bigoted sociopath, a jihadi terrorist, or anyone of a kind that desire absolute victory over others. Such people accept definitions of success popularised by wizards of propaganda that ask them to destroy rivals, and hence propagate the divisive splintering of society.

* * *

Popular norms would have us believe that those who possess the most in social trophies are winners in life. This means society constantly reinforces the idea that 'average' people are undeserving, and cannot feel a sense of fulfilment. There is constant pressure to play catch up. Instead, what if we realise that everyone, quite matter-of-factly, is average or 'lacking' at something or the other? At the risk of sounding iconoclastic—even movie stars, Olympic athletes, and Presidents of nations are average. All of us are human and fallible, and *average* in many aspects.

> Being 'average' in some respects, and whole-heartedly accepting this about others and ourselves, helps in living life to the fullest, without feeling that something is lacking.

We should attach no stigma to the word *average*. It is not about professing, 'I am humble,' and then being maleficent like Dickens' character Uriah Heep, in the classic *David Copperfield*. It is about feeling blessed, equitable and a part of humanity. Being 'average' in some respects, and whole-heartedly accepting this about others and ourselves, helps in living life to the fullest, without feeling that something is lacking. It has nothing to do with our possessions, performance or pride. Can you look at yourself, be modest and believe you are average, and still feel blessed and unique? Such an insight, when recognised volitionally and applied without bias, would bolster a resilient self-esteem.

* * *

A related insight I had was that nature and civilisation will seem inherently unfair if we base our sense of justice on the popular, instead of the personal. The 'winners' want the rest to believe that life is a game in which the best things are only for the best players. This is the only way they can label their position as winners, or as the 'best', regardless of whether the value they have to offer is commensurate or questionable. We will feel inadequate if we base our success and state of mind on popularly touted benefits of competing alone.

Consider that a premium car, an elaborate house, or expensive holidays are among the ways you feel others are at an advantage. This then, is a way that makes you feel *you are a loser*…and you *are* a loser—when you stick to these terms. The collective mnemonic's fallacy of defining success on the wrong ideals has left a major percentage of society feeling inadequate and yearning for more. It is impossible for the 'top percentage' to be permanently content too. Our usual definitions of success constantly shift the standards in regard to what we should be, do or have. The collective mnemonic seems to house, in addition to its cues, the idea that we have no choice, and that we *have* to play the social game of competing and comparison. It harbours an incorrect version of winning.

Competition exists, fair and foul. We cannot dismiss destructive conflict and rabid competition. These have to be accepted. But, a personal competitive philosophy will create proactive terms for us to learn the uncommon, and yet, accept the common, in the ways of winning and losing. This philosophy, I believe, can support us in recognising our own niche success.

Initially Nachiket had it figured out, and felt his ability, adequate effort and the 'known' ways of justice would produce favourable results. There was no need to doubt the volumes of literature, both fiction and non-fiction, that had declared 'proven' ways to succeed. Perhaps armed with academic learning, we feel reason and order rule supreme. However, when a person who is only academically tutored becomes aware, he might see the environment as extremely critical and unfairly competitive. I confess that it was far beyond anything I had imagined from within the safety of my home and academia.

Most people, on becoming aware, quickly toe the line of popular social protocol, or they may accept what they may feel is a laidback lifestyle and profession. They may feel all the while, regardless of their choosing that what they are is inadequate. There is an alternative proactive attitude we can develop instead. This attitude would help us realise and accept, without any doubt, that we get what we deserve. And, that we can feel deserving of this much and more without feeling pressured by what others have, now or ever.

Two academicians, Charles Darwin and Adam Smith, seem to suggest, directly or indirectly, that competitiveness and comparison are inherent in society, and that they are essential survival mechanisms. Popular thought claims 'The best succeed,' as the message of these stalwarts. Our age hence emphasises competition and winning to such a degree that it is easily misunderstood. We have already discussed the stupidity of taking Darwin's theory of evolution in an illiterate species, and applying them to the literate and civilised human race (the example of the drone bee[18]). Further, Adam Smith's perfect markets, in which competition and meritocracy are almost synonymous, do not hold water. Many of our markets suppress entities that can add commendable value to society. Many genuine players may be suppressed because they lack the 'cash' or the 'right connections' to sustain or continue. Adam Smith made us believe that resources are scarce, and Darwin said only the environmentally fittest survive. 'Scramble and fight for the crumbs,' they seemed to say. What people have forgotten is—there is probably enough for all on the table. Externalities like the media, the market, and (tongue-in-cheek) the mother-in-law control your wants instead!

✳ ✳ ✳

Historical urges have seeded a trait in several people that I call 'one-upmanship'. Commonly, many people in their efforts to be one-up pay lip-service to human equality, while blatantly disregarding human dignity and individual self-esteem. One-upmanship is an outward

---

[18]   As explained earlier, the genitalia of a mating drone bee explode and inject the virgin queen bee with sperm, also effectively plugging her up from all other male drones' sperm

expression of a strong need to establish relative superiority. Present-day advertising exemplifies—and perhaps legitimises—this one-upmanship. Most advertising tries to create a sense of inadequacy or 'need' in the buyer, usually in relation to another, to force a buying decision. Some advertisers also put down competing products instead of just promoting the pluses of whatever they are pitching. To be superior, as the word implies, requires *relative* measures. However, we are not talking of goods and services here, but thinking, feeling beings. A survival strategy that is based purely on the conquest of others is likely to translate to damaging human competition.

Competing in the common vein also advocates the kind of 'killer instinct' popularised by sport. This promotes the instinct to vanquish, or have no mercy. Take for example the practice of 'sledging' in the game of cricket. This practice aims at using personal taunts to get into the minds of the opponents and unsettle them. Children who play the game sometimes see sledging as acceptable, but cheating as not. Some people carry the 'killer instinct' outside the sports arena. For people who are innocent theorists, or are blind to life as it really is, experiencing this 'killer instinct' can be a shock and a challenge. They wake up to the fact that it can be a wild-world where 'it's hard to get by just upon a smile.'[19]

I notice that popular thought in this aggressive age seems to tout one-upmanship and the killer instinct. Many see these traits as enhancing the chances of success. Individuals soaked in these twisted qualities waste effort in thinking up original ways to unnerve their opponents.

---

[19]    From the song "Wild World" by the British singer-songwriter Cat Stevens aka Yusuf

They are blind to benefit-
ing from developing their
own skills, or from any
value-addition they can
bring. They generally create avenues to gain un-
fairly; using warped traits

> When we compete to win instead of competing to deliver excellence, one-upmanship and the killer instinct become tools.

like intimidation and opportunism, instead of allowing
effort and value to get its just dues. When we compete to
win instead of competing to deliver excellence, one-upmanship and the killer instinct become tools. These tools
could throw the uninitiated off-balance.

Competition is useful to deliver excellence. However,
this idea of merit may take a back seat when winning
is the only incentive. There is pressure created by a
focus on winning alone, by the idea that second place
is for the first loser. Nature tells us to block rivals in
evolution. The collective understanding indoctrinates
us with the idea that competing aggressively is the only
way to success. Strong urges to compete destructively
and to win decisively, therefore, exist. Both the illiterate
natural force and a collective confusion on the idea of
competition promote such urges. Such influences have
no tempering framework as in a true sport. This causes
people to consider foul means on par with the fair.

✳ ✳ ✳

Life generally maximises differences in opportunity—
unlike sport, which provides a level playing field. I
speculate, a little tentatively, that games or sports came
about in the following ways. They could have been

invented for entertaining adults, or as an offshoot of toys to keep children occupied. They could have also originated as training exercises to keep men prepared for battle. Another possibility is that they could have developed from gory practices, such as public hangings in medieval times and throwing of slaves to the lions in the Roman era.

Historically, games seem to have come about as a distraction for the general public. The upper classes felt it was dangerous for the masses to realise they were being short-changed by the social order. They created distractions to keep the focus away from their wrongdoings and maintain status quo in the social pecking order. A select few champions are showcased with a boy/girl next-door aura, which seems to imply that anybody from the masses can make it. All the while, the 'powers that be' are gently pushing an elitist agenda; a separation that promises select benefits solely for being one-up. Such a discriminatory game of life keeps providing distracting crumbs and promises, based on relative stature, while subtly imposing one-upmanship.

Sports *can* be compared to life, but for a different reason—the antithesis of their purported end. Sports are good because they teach us sportsmanship. They teach us that losing can be fair, and is not the end of the world. Sporting champions lose, sometimes more often than they win. They still inspire us to newer successes and

> In real life, there is nobody to knock into a bloody pulp; there are no championships to win, and no trophies to flaunt.

better things without loss of heart. That is the only par-allel to life. In real life, there is nobody to knock into a bloody pulp; there are no championships to win, and no trophies to flaunt, as in games and sports.

The common reaction to such a statement will usually be disagreement. This is because years of conditioning by a sensationalist media have caused us to liken life to sports. They promote the obsession to be ahead, which can be an unnecessary and troublesome mindset for the long haul. It is a popularly promoted addiction, which is hard to kick. Many people forsake common civilities for the prize because of a conditioning that life is a frivolous game anyway. We need to overcome the spurious licence, which conditions us to treat life as only a game. When we acknowledge there are many non-competitive issues in life that require our attention, we become more caring and considerate. Most of us do see sports positively, and remain aware that they are for fitness, camaraderie and entertainment. The idea is we play 'No games, just sports!'[20] We don't indulge in damaging acts or play unnerving 'games' to stay ahead. While we can keep the progressive aspects of the analogy between sports and life, we must yet avoid treating life as 'Just a game!'[21]

---

[20]    A fictitious tagline for a sports shoe from the movie *What Women Want* (2000)

[21]    A remarkable departure from the norm, but one which nonetheless demonstrates that sport is bigger than just a game, is reflected in Dr Vijay Barse's movement in India, slum soccer. The ultimate aim of the slum soccer network is reaching out to the Indian homeless using football as a tool for social improvement and empowerment. Visit http://www.slumsoccer.org

Organisations too may be ruthless in their pursuit of success. They may lack a higher and humane purpose. The 1975 Norman Jewison film, *Rollerball*, depicted this. In this film, monopolistic corporations of the future promote a ruthless and bloody full contact game—yes, a game—called Rollerball as the prime distraction for the masses. There are no governments, no wars and no crime, just corporations and Rollerball. Nonetheless, a scene from the film shows a spectator clawing at the wire net around the arena, screaming at the blood and gore in the pit: 'A game? Is that what it's meant to be? A game?'

The Hindu epic, *The Mahabharata*, is a narration of the internecine conflict between two ruling clans, the Pandavs and the Kauravs. One of its principal characters, Duryodhan, a Kaurav, develops a deep hatred for his cousins, the Pandavs. The Pandavs had laughed at Duryodhan's clumsiness, which he saw as a jibe referring to his blind father. This deep-seated hatred prevents Duryodhan from seeing reason and sharing the throne. He brings about the destruction of his entire clan, the Kauravs, because of his stubbornness.

A person like Duryodhan has a paranoid disposition and a personality complex, which interferes with the ability to think rationally. Most of us brush aside incidents like people laughing at us with an attitude reflected in the statement 'Rubber glue, back to you.' We could feel some discomfort for a bit, but we steer clear of being bogged down. Duryodhan was constantly troubled because he depended on artificial props. He wanted to be the sole heir to the throne to feel complete. Duryodhan's enmity with the Pandavs stemmed from an unreasonable competitive attitude, a need to deprive and be one-up. His attitude is a reflection of what competition should not be. Competing purely to establish relative superiority or inferiority in our lives, as in a game, never leads to a positive conclusion.

We can rise above any propaganda that make us feel whatever we are or have is inadequate. One-upmanship and the killer instinct will stop affecting us when we change the yardsticks by which we measure our success. When we focus on doing our best and celebrating personal successes, the power we feel is tremendous. Motivation with an external focus on winning and losing is self-defeating. Motivation that makes you want to better yourself and your situation, all the while leading to *personal* successes, is self-sustaining. Dr Dharmaraj was trying to ignite this sense in Nachiket, who was at heart, thinking on a relative plane. Dharmaraj attempted to convey to Nachiket that people are worthy of their own successes, and do not need to imitate or compare themselves with anyone else. They need not feel superior or inferior.

A caution to be aware of at this point is that the conventionally accomplished may refuse this version of competition as discouraging. One must add for our flag-bearers, winning *does* matter. Nobody is attempting to steal your thunder. Nevertheless, common standards of glory are likely to be transient without constant positive strokes to the psyche. A sense of inadequacy from losing stature can sap the energy to perform when using only a win or lose perspective. What matters is to feel better every time, in some measure or the other. When people say 'winning is everything,' we should take it to really mean—*find success in everything*. With the right mindset, we can come to the surprising realisation that winning is not a principal result, as is commonly touted. Winning is a by-product. If we focus our energy on improving in some respect or another, even in small increments, the outcomes would be outstanding, in some respect or another. We would always look back at where we were and where we are now with equanimity.

Despite popular beliefs about winning and losing in the game of life, it is too real to be so lightly discounted. Life is not a game when 95 per cent of our population could be suffering from put-downs by the remaining 5 [22]. It is not a game if we feel forced to crave tokens of superior status. It is not a game when innocent children grow up believing that they have to be better than the Joneses. It is not a game when we look at life, based on trophies acquired, instead of cherishing what you have achieved *for the inner you*. In

> Despite popular beliefs about winning and losing in the game of life, it is too real to be so lightly discounted.

---

[22] See CNBC's Reporter and Editor Robert Frank's article titled *Who me? A One Percenter* dated 26th July 2012, on the extent of the skew and misconceptions as regards affluence.

this apparent selfishness and clichéd objective is the inspiration to adopt a larger personal cause beyond the self; a cause which would be rewarding *per se*.

✳ ✳ ✳

What then is healthy competition? Do we feel at a competitive disadvantage when we wake up to a challenging environment? Do we fight because of our chosen disagreement (or agreement), or just to be superior? Is this alternative of personal betterment too much to consider? Is it too hard to believe that a personal, yet all-encompassing intent can be a successful strategy? Sure it is hard. Nachiket is also sceptical. But really, the degree of comfort we attain when we let go of relative yardsticks in life is phenomenal. There are other valid and more enduring concepts to live by. What constitutes valid competition in which you can win or lose without depriving or feeling deprived? We see this next.

### *Section Highlights:*

- The first and foremost complication in the jumbled bag of theory is the ideas in it with regard to winning and competition.
- Time has twisted Darwin and Adam Smith's macro-theories of 'survival of the fittest' and 'competitive markets' to apply them in the micro to individuals. This twisting has fashioned a society that feels justified in using any means to win.
- The social environment of this age does not always support merit and justice. It lacks a level playing field unlike sports.

- One can hypothesise there is a hidden elitist agenda in society driving it to promote an inequitable pecking order.
- This elitism encourages relative stature and sidelines challenges to the status quo.
- When we anchor in absolute personal betterment instead of relative victories, we drop a lot of unnecessary mental baggage.
- We achieve this by realising the uselessness of comparing ourselves with others when it comes to our self-esteem.

## THE BONA FIDE BATTLE

Are the factors that commonly motivate us to compete incorrect? What is clear to me is we usually compete for a better world of our own—professional, personal, and social. Most people conclude that these things have to be relative, and that we have to compete for a higher relative position. Many also see conflict amongst different social sub-groups, and compete to establish the superiority of their beliefs. One can acknowledge that what we believe to be good and bad is not absolute, and that many things have a degree of both. What is legal in one country could be illegal in another. Prostitution is legal in Thailand as of now, and illegal almost the world over. Similarly, a cancer patient may ingest marijuana legally in some parts of the USA[23]. The Pope pardoned the eating of human flesh by plane-crash victims in an

---

[23] Recently, two US states, Washington and Colorado, have voted to permit 'recreational' use of marijuana, in contravention of Federal law

extraordinary case. Sometimes the correct thing to do insofar as our employer is concerned might be wrong in the eyes of several others (Imagine being a pro-tobacco lobbyist). How do we recognise the right conflict to pick, and develop the appropriate competitive spirit?

As suggested in the section 'The Yellow Brick Road', we base our actions on inner spirit and intent. To me, the right compet- itive spirit depends on having a clear personal intent as to what needs to get better because of

> Aligning our competitive drive to a broadly generic intent, which nonetheless is in line with a personal purpose, would allow us to tap into non-conflicting energies and result in durable success.

our action. With the correct intent, we would feel at ease with our effort and its results. Aligning our competitive drive to a broadly generic intent, which nonetheless is in line with a personal purpose, would allow us to tap into non-conflicting energies and result in durable success. Ironically, it is a *personal* perspective that makes the com- petition we face generic. No single person (or persons) in any frame of time or space causes the need to compete. Our true struggle may not be with another person or en- tity, but with a situation that is ours and ours alone. This is what Dharmaraj wanted Nachiket to understand.

✳ ✳ ✳

We can ask—why do some struggles and conflicts from competing seem unending or indeterminable, sometimes with unjust, inadequate or delayed results, even in conclusion? I attempt here, a pseudo-scientific stab at explaining 'indeterminism' and 'uncertainty' in the results of our actions. This explanation includes ideas from quantum physics and Einstein's thinking in a simplistic manner, having no other basis, but speculation. The model can be easily pooh-poohed, but does offer an unusual perspective to reflect on.

The figure (Pic. 2—A Representation of Uncertainty in Creation) represents action percolating down to the building blocks (quanta) of Creation. These building blocks are in the core of Creation where time is notional. The core is an amalgamation of matter, energy, space and time. Reactions, in the form of consequences or connected external events, could be from this core. A person could experience the reactions in a different time and space from that of his action. This explanation is not just a leap of faith. We *are* aware that some events happen quite randomly. We attribute them to chance.

Pic 2. A Representation of Uncertainty in Creation



Imagine, for example, a narrow escape on a pedestrian crossing. A car almost hits you. Suppose we had some way of knowing all the relevant details of the car that missed you. The car that should have hit you at the intersection, and to which you gave a one-finger salute before going your way, was fractionally late and missed you because of a faulty fuel injection system that should have been rectified a week ago—and, which *would* have been rectified if the driver of the car had not fallen ill, and postponed the fixing. Well, you get the drift! The question is, 'What is chance?' Is something at an intangible core triggering what we face in the tangible? Do the rules at the miniature quantum level affect a larger being? Are there upward or downward causations between the small and the large, between the gross and the subtle? Is this what chance is? Why you? We leave the questions begging...

To understand conflict is personally specific, and perhaps of our own making, consider a somewhat abstract concept. Karma is the Hindu and Buddhist belief, which many interpret to be the underlying principle that makes actions rebound as consequences or results. Actions are both influenced by, and the result of, karma. Actions are in themselves neutral, but the intent of the initiator causes a karmic 'load'. This is hard to grasp. We generally do not attribute chance happenings to a detached God, aliens from outer space, or a mad experiment in which we are networked to a reality simulator. Still, conflicts and happenings we experience could have causes elsewhere in the space-time continuum, as suggested in the Uncertainty model.

This Uncertainty model is compatible with the Karmic principle. It supports the argument that we lack any exact, controllable, or focused basis for conflict (and competition). A greater whole possibly decides these. If our actions drop into a core where time is also indeterminate, then in addition to our actions, we may face consequences from something larger and beyond time. I can only suggest that the consequences of one's

> Our actions should therefore consider, to the extent feasible, that everyone and everything matters.

deeds are from a wider spectrum of things. Personal action should include something larger to influence this greater whole. Our actions should therefore consider, to the extent feasible, that everyone and everything matters. The karmic backlash could be a result of misplaced egoism, a lack of concern for anything else other than oneself.

Granted, this may setup grounds for the convoluted question, 'Are we really helping others when the intent is to benefit ourselves?' The answer is in the question itself. Results are wholly dependent on the *intent* during the act. When people drop egoistic seeds into the deeper core, they will reap inhibited or no rewards, even if the actions seem constructive. If the intent is larger, more caring of bigger concerns, and aimed at helping others or at adding constructive value, the results are likely to be more tangible and progressive… somewhere… sometime. We will progress without guilt, fear or any other form of unease.

Whether this kind of Uncertainty model or Karma actually exists may be incidental to the discussion. It only helps in clarifying that there are certain things that happen to us for which there can be no ready explanation. But, you cannot tell people they lack control of their lives when they are experiencing life's highs. It is also hard to accept that any struggle we face is a result of some unknown quantum effects or karma. We overlook such possibilities in favour of palpable, immediate and controllable effects. This is mostly because of our awareness of, and respect for, free will. Free will is alive and well. Here is how we could look at it.

Consider that there exists an intelligent divide between what we meet and how we meet it. Let us distinguish between Fate and Destiny. Fate is what you meet or encounter, and destiny is a result of how it is met[24]. What we do creates destiny, and the environment we are in, or face, is fate. The doorbell rings, and we are ignorant of who is on the other side of the door. That is fate (what you meet). Whether we choose to open the door or not is destiny (how you meet it). Now a twist: The fate or reality met by us could be caused by externalities outside individual control. What we do in turn affects the fate of others and, to a certain extent, how the external world unfolds. The caller's choice—the destiny he fabricated—was to ring the doorbell, and this became our fate—a situation to face. Similarly, when we choose to open the door, this decision becomes the fate of the person on the other side of the door.

The final twist, consider that our actions could create options for others to choose from, and thus we contribute to *creating that fate which we face*. By

---

[24]    Swami Chinmayananda (1916–93)

keeping your light on, a handy doorbell button, and not hanging a 'Do Not Disturb' sign, you created options that allowed the doorbell to be rung. When the person at the door rang the doorbell, he created the options for you to choose whether to open the door, shout 'Get lost!' or to sit as quiet as a mouse, and wait for the person to go away. In this example, the action of ringing the doorbell triggered only one set of possible transactions. You could potentially create all the options for others' choices. *Our choices create options from which others choose.* THIS IS THE COMPLETE UNCERTAINTY OR KARMIC CYCLE.

We, in fact, will face a future in whose creation we can (and possibly do) play a significant part. Also, we are what we are and where we are, because of options that we presented to others. Our today is the result of many options we created, somewhere… sometime… from which others chose—options that we may *be ignorant of, or have forgotten creating*. This then is what Dharmaraj meant to convey as regards what we can and cannot control when he said, 'When you create enough options for others to choose from, you are able to influence their decisions.'

> Our today is the result of many options we created, somewhere… sometime… from which others chose—options that we may be ignorant of or have forgotten creating.

What *are* we competing with then? We are not in competition with one another, as in a game or sport. People appear to be grappling with each other because of an *a priori* framework set by a mad scheme of *civilisation*. We believe we are in conflict with *one another* when in reality we are only facing our own unique situation. Competition is how we dialogue with our fate and create our destiny. Destiny helps our fate turn out to be better and vice-versa. We can create our destiny from this point forward and pre-empt any adverse fate to a degree. Nachiket saw competition and conflict as thrust upon him. We can instead, see it as a unique situation in which to take ownership. It is us, our situation, what we care about, and nothing or no one else in the ultimate analysis. There is nothing relative. This then is the bona fide battle.

How do we relate to this concept of unique standing? Is it pompous to think one's life or anyone's life in general, is as relevant as the lives of those renowned or accomplished by common measures? Is it correct to demolish all that we have learned about excellence in competition and about the need to win? Is life not about being better than what others are? Despite such a personal philosophy on competition sounding selfish, and additionally, as closing our eyes to achievement, the real essence of such a perspective is in consonance with a larger result orientation. This involves developing a sense of belonging to something larger, without the need to be 'superior' relative to others.

Our need to be on top of all others seems to be a part of the collective mnemonic's tenets. This is also the undoing from living collaboratively as a race. We find it hard to tolerate other beliefs, leave alone celebrate different schools of thought. However, when we broaden our vision to distinguish between constructive and destructive ideas, unbiased by their origin, we can find the ability to rejoice together. This is possible, if and only if, we include all others in our sense of success. It requires us to have humility when it comes to interaction with others, and yet have a sense of uniqueness in terms of our self-esteem. The ability to convert self-esteem to action, ignoring any conflicting gibes and barbs is the next step. How? We will look at this in a forthcoming chapter.

As you proceed, you would be able to accept that 'the point of power is [undeniably] in the present moment.' Things can change. You can override the programming that complying with popular definitions of winning is the only way to live. You can *win* by your own standards, with your own purpose, and according to the values that concern you. It is hard to change all that we have learned about winning as individuals and as part of a larger group. Nachiket was having a hard time, as was evident from his incessant questions. However, when we replace desires to win using relative standards by an absolute, yet constructive one, a lot of mental overhead just ceases to exist.

> You can win by your own standards, with your own purpose, and according to the values that concern you.

✳ ✳ ✳

Your first key principle of the book—a mantra to be emblazoned in gold in your mind—is 'Meet your fate; make your destiny.' We may not be able to choose what we meet. Accept this with as much matter-of-factness as you do the fact you are alive. Drop the relative measure and accept yourself—right here, right now. Not all that has happened was in your control, and you control all that will happen only with an uncertain karmic bias. Accept karmic and quantum influence over anything, and perhaps all things. But also, take control of how you meet what you face. Apply effort to the best of your abilities, faculties and wit.

Rest a while and consider that the selections of others, among options we created for them to choose from, causes everything we face; some known options… some unknown. Pause and think how much more accomplished we can be if, instead of comparing, we draw on a sense of passion for just getting better and better… improving our personal best in some facet or manner. Become truly concerned with bettering what concerns you. Show up… and act on your concerns. The rest just happens. Now is a good time to wake up and live with personal awareness, accept fate and carve your destiny.

✳ ✳ ✳

People feel defenceless if they have to change suddenly. How do I change with the baggage of a reckless past, or a limited fortune, or an on-going testing situation? We can skill ourselves to ease the transition to a better progressive world of our own. The 'Good Living Practices' [GLP's] at the end of the book will help do this. The first of the GLPs to visit now is 'Flying Above the Flak'. This provides a method to manage fear. This GLP should also help in dealing with critical and competitive environments that attempt to intimidate. We can take steps to be proactive by first managing fear. This helps us move in the direction of an empowered, rational and personal purpose.

### *Section Highlights:*

- Our dreams need to be for things larger than just us, while still being incomparably personal and inspiring.
- True competition, which gets progressive results, is not from conflict with, or victory over, any person or entity. It is a measure of our response-ability in facing our *own* unique situation.
- We can set our own unique personal benchmarks without seeing ourselves as being in conflict with others.
- Competing effectively is all about an ability to create enough options for others to choose from, improving the odds of their choices bringing about the results we desire.
- Causative reactions from a subtle core as well as the person's intent at the time of action, not action alone, determine if the exact desired results materialise.
- If our intentions are caring, considerate and helpful, and, we include others in our sense of success, progressive results will occur appropriately.

**5**

# IN-SANITY

'What happened to me?' Nachiket demanded to know, after a few uneventful sessions. The sessions had not seemed any different. However, Dr Dharmaraj realised that Nachiket had gradually ceased addressing him as divine. He had thought Nachiket would work his way up to such a question after gradually developing insight, but there it was, all of a sudden. The doctor decided it was time for psycho-education and told Nachiket the truth.

'To be honest, we don't know yet. There is evidence of neurotransmitters, the chemicals that carry information from one brain nerve cell to the other, being involved. Too much of these chemicals in certain areas of the brain cause it to malfunction. The good news is that it is partly due to such a chemical imbalance, despite the mental manifestation… and that you are responding to the medication.'

'Then what about all I still sense…and my suspicions? It seems valid and coherent,' Nachiket asked, puzzled.

'The brain has a funny way of rationalising,' The doctor explained. 'It thinks in patterns. Even if something strange happens, it forces itself to try and detect a pattern. That is why all you experienced seemed valid.'

'Am I ill?' Nachiket inquired.

'You are not so much ill as confused,' Dharmaraj reassured him. 'It is a combination of factors from physiology, social conditions, stress and innate sensitivity that trigger such symptoms. Perhaps you are as ill as a person with diabetes or high blood pressure, though the comparison is not very accurate. Medication may help, but it may not be the only curative measure.'

'I don't know how to think without my beliefs, my perceptions of a different way of communication, and, the conclusions I have reached,' declared Nachiket.

'Let's look at these,' said Dr Dharmaraj. 'Don't debate if the perceptions are real or not. Just ask yourself, are they helpful? Can they help you to live happily and productively with others?' Dharmaraj paused. Nachiket's answer could mean the difference between developing the intent to recover, and continuing to wallow in his contorted thinking. The answer came slowly.

'I think…it…could be… No, it is not right. Such beliefs do not help in productive and constructive living. However, some of it still seems strangely valid…' Nachiket responded.

Dharmaraj was relieved. Nachiket was seeing a glimmer of reason despite the continuing symptoms. 'The symptoms of this condition influence you greatly.

When you couple this with the inherent ambiguity of symbols and language—and body language—it is normal to feel confused.'

'I felt all of Creation was focused on me alone. I felt like I was the centre of the Universe. And now everything is wrong!' exclaimed Nachiket.

'There is success in this, not the apparent failure you perceive.' Dharmaraj said animatedly. 'It will take some time, but let me assure you, those who have gone through this condition and recovered are in many ways better equipped now. It may seem clichéd, but you will see that tough times don't last, tough people do!'

'But all that understanding…the feeling people were trying to communicate in radically different ways…' said Nachiket.

'For several people, such a different communication style could be from their choosing it as the right way to function,' Dr Dharmaraj explained, referring to cues such as body postures that some people use in interactions. 'Some may not be aware, that they are using such a style. Both spurious and valid communication styles, do exist. Many find it difficult to differentiate the spurious from the valid. Often, they manifest in a metaphorical fashion and this makes it hard to decipher. For some, the cues may seem hostile and aggressive instead of collaborative, when first perceived. You did not see such patterns earlier. Perhaps you were too self-absorbed and without trust. Now that you have awakened and become aware, you will be a better judge of what is valid and what is not.'

'When I look back at what happened to me, I see a progression of suspicions and doubts,' agreed Nachiket. 'I still don't see how I will fit in with other people.'

'Typically, because of our internal focus, we fail to notice the things that will help us get along in society. Experts claim that only seven per cent of what is understood depends on the explicitly stated. We base a large portion of what we understand on tone and visual cues such as body language. When you perceive this, or interact with an aggressive individual, you may feel ill equipped. However, if you firmly believe in a growing personal purpose, you will not be intimidated. You will be proactive and take the learning life has to offer. Everything, including the unusual patterns, will be grist to your mill.' Dr Dharmaraj was trying hard to make the transition easier.

Nachiket sounded miffed. 'But many others seem "awake" to these aspects of Creation much before me. My parents never taught me all this. Isn't this unfair?'

'Honestly, Nachiket,' said the doctor, 'there is nothing to teach. Nobody, your parents included, can force awareness. These aspects are very personal and learnt by observation.'

'When I see the time I have lost, I feel I can never make up. My schoolmates are in better positions than I am. I could have lost the race,' said Nachiket, resorting once again to relative measures.

Dharmaraj reminded him, 'Again, why do you feel you should be measured by the success of others? You have a unique learning that is yours and yours alone. We will talk about this next time. Relax for a bit now. Think about your learning. Review your notes. Just think of the time lost as a sabbatical in which you were learning something special. We spoke a little on personally unique goals. We will talk more on this the next time around.'

This was a sign of a breakthrough, the kind that the doctor had been waiting for. Nachiket had begun to see that the delusional patterns he had experienced could be wrong. The medications were acting well, the hallucinations were receding, and he was gaining more focus. Nevertheless, the happy ending could still be far away. The doctor added a mild anti-depressant to his prescription to combat any adverse feelings Nachiket might dwell on as he gained insight. The doctor told the parents to encourage conversation and give Nachiket small, achievable and everyday tasks around the house.

## THE SURROGATE SENSE

Now for the second problem that is hypothesised to affect the psyche, faulty cues from the collective mnemonic. The collective mnemonic is unintelligent, but it seems to have enough artistic sense to suggest imaginary connections. It pushes the mind to derive meanings in random stimuli, attempting to make sense of assorted symbols. The arrangements perceived may have artistic sense and appeal, in what can be likened to a kaleidoscopic concoction of symbols. But on the other hand, they may be disturbing. If our mind imparts connectivity to the random, which is neither rational nor artistic, we may end up wondering, 'What *is* this?' This kind of connectivity, when sensed, can cause havoc if we don't have plausible explanations for the phenomenon.

We know that language is a great gift, and the mind, a wonderful instrument. However, the mind's ability to detect patterns and derive meaning sometimes acts against us. When the detections of the mind are deviant, it could lead to strange conclusions, out-of-sync with a larger context. Some aspects—disembodied stimuli, body language, double entendre, chance happenings and coincidences that people sometimes experience—may confuse us. Such aspects force reactions bordering on superstition. Knowing how our minds deviate from reason can help us to be contextual, and prevent mystical meandering. We will add a demystifying understanding in this chapter. This understanding would help rise above 'disorienters' that show up when self-absorption combines with an overactive imagination; a common trait of schizophrenia. You will see how bizarre the world of the flawed collective mnemonic can get. Be cautioned, we will be walking a thin line between the rational and the irrational.

> Knowing how our minds deviate from reason can help us to be contextual, and prevent mystical meandering.

* * *

What makes for schizophrenia? How can one prepare to face surreal challenges such as feeling that others can read one's mind? As discussed earlier—different environments, foreign lands, different cultures and social paradigms, or new relationships are a part of life. Any new reality could challenge our comfortable cocoon of explanations. Some people attempt to figure a way back using only known rules and logic, especially if they go largely by theory. Most of us attempt to understand any novel experiences using our current learning alone. Some, like Nachiket, reach spurious conclusions, as what they know cannot explain what they perceive.

The collective mnemonic in a person's psyche may cause stressful generalisations of conflict. Issues such as the erstwhile Cold War, or the fear of God, spirits, or nuclear oblivion, and fear of authority are among the many conflicts in which an afflicted person could feel entangled. Such conflicts can be a foundation for some bizarre types of connectivity and communication. For example, they may cause a sensitive individual to connect various published articles and believe that an elaborate conspiracy is at work. The Hollywood movie, *A Beautiful Mind* portrays this. The film is based, even if loosely, on the true story of American Nobel laureate John Nash, a person afflicted with schizophrenia, in a book with the same name[26]. It shows him looking for coded messages to spies in common news articles.

Similarly, a deeply religious individual could see divine messages in everyday happenings. The overly sensitive often create an artificial, and sometimes delusional, framework of explanations for their unusual perceptions. Stressed 'normal' persons may see peculiar meanings in a normal environment too. It is often not a conscious reaction. For example, the not so vulnerable, when stressed, could be sensitive to events such as a black cat crossing their path. When a person relies predominantly on a kind of surrogate sense for decisions, it would cause behaviour that seems insane or eccentric.

---

[26]    Nasar, Sylvia. *A Beautiful Mind.* Simon & Schuster Paperbacks, print.

How does this happen? I ask you to consider that the brain's frontal lobe could automatically link random experiences and events in a person's vicinity[27]. It tends to attach everything in the vicinity to whatever is uppermost or innermost in the mind. The afflicted individual lives with a strange connectivity, imaginatively associating the environment, the corporal, and the mental. For some, these connections are deviant. A simple example: The entry of a person named Roger into a room could cause a stressed and sensitive individual to make a deviant connection. Pressed for time, he immediately approves a proposal under discussion. He does this because 'Roger' is military jargon for 'Okay,' and not because of the contextual merit of the proposal.

> The afflicted individual lives with a strange connectivity, imaginatively linking the environment, the corporal, and the mental.

The mind can also derive surrogate meaning lacking common reason in other ways. There is a strange rationality during dreaming where the nonsensical seems sensible. During REM (Rapid Eye Movement) sleep, the state when we dream, the frontal lobe does what it is best at doing: giving coherence to randomness. This leads to the dream's apparent continuity, keeping the dreamer in the dream and asleep. However, if we impart dream-like associations and inferences to random happenings in a waking state, it is a deviant condition.

---

[27]   Some research points to the limbic cortex and not the frontal lobe as the place from which the most primal and random connectivity could emerge.

Trace back a random train of thought in a waking state to help you see what this means. A chain of thought could end in topics far removed from its trigger. For example, an advertising billboard for shoes reminds you that you left in a hurry and did not polish your shoes, despite a business meeting. Then, you think of the business proposal you made for the meeting last night, and then, your child's homework. You recall that you could lend no help to your child because of the business proposal you had to make. The distinction between such a normal chain of thinking and an odd chain is in the mix-up of its perceived intent. An afflicted person could interpret the failure to help the child as *the* insinuation of the advertisement.

A phenomenon along similar lines is *synchronicity*. Synchronicity is an occurrence with very little formal research. In its vanilla form, synchronicity is merely noticeable coincidence. Carl Jung has speculated that it is an 'acausal connecting principle' between dreams and the real world. Dr Remo Roth, a psychologist in Zurich, who provides an interesting collection of information at a German website, has this to say about Jung in an English translation of his site[28].

'When one observes one's dreams over a longer period, one becomes aware that often, outward events occur that are very similar to the content of one's dreams. It would seem that the inner world and the outer world coincide. Carl G. Jung had suggested that one should, instead of looking for a magical relationship as they did in mediaeval times; try to find the common meaning of such relatively simultaneous inner and

---

[28]     www.psychovision.ch

outer events. The principle that underlies this nexus, he called *synchronicity*.

Jung cites in his letters [Jung, 1973, p. 395] an occurrence that is an impressive example of synchronicity: 'For instance, I walk with a woman patient in the woods. She tells me about the first dream in her life that had made an everlasting impression upon her. She had seen a spectral fox coming down the stairs in her parental home. At this moment, a real fox comes out of the trees about forty yards away and walks quietly on the path ahead of us for several minutes. The animal behaves as if it were a partner in the human situation.'

According to Jung, it would be wrong and extremely dangerous to see a causal relationship between the two occurrences, and to say that one event was the cause of the other. That would be nothing other than a relapse to the magical-causal thinking of the middle ages. Instead of this, we must accept that the two occurrences are not causally connected, but rather by a common meaning. This means that we have to extract the implication of the symbol 'fox' for the interpretation of this synchronicity. This would somehow purport, that the dreamer herself—metaphorically speaking—should be led much more by her 'inner fox,' meaning that she must recover the instinctive cleverness [ingenuity] she had lost with her intellectual point of view.

Jung's example, quoted by Dr Roth, interprets a causal trait (ingenuity) for an occurrence that is otherwise claimed 'acausal'. Jung's interpretation is a helpful conclusion. There is a tacit assumption in the example that people experience synchronicity without seeing it as hostile or isolating. Persons with schizophrenia, however, could perceive such instances as hostile. If people, whether afflicted or normal, cannot interpret these instances as helpful aids, it is better in the interest of our sanity not to read any meaning into them at all. There is no reason to believe there is meaning in the event, or that it has a context pertinent to the individual. It is what it is—an interpretation of coincidence. The event is open to multiple interpretations. This could lead to many a wild fox, I mean, wild goose chase!

✳ ✳ ✳

Pic 3. Connectivity: An Example

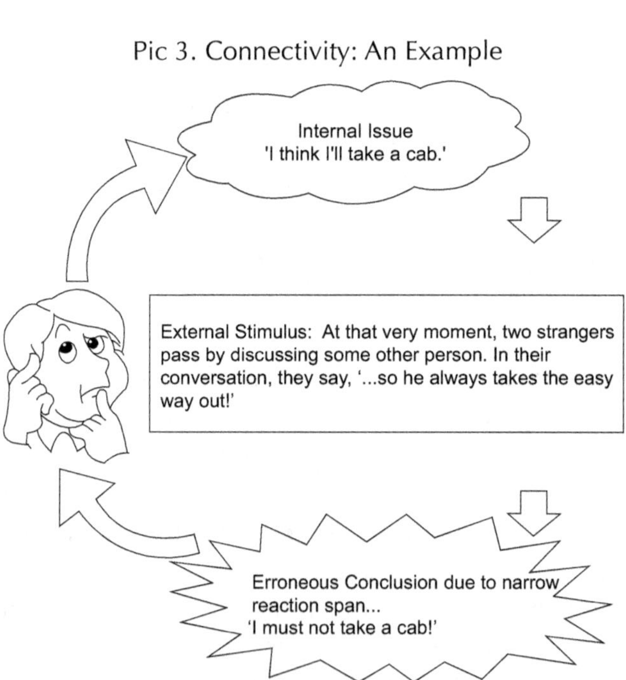


When under stress, a person may interpret random activity in the environment as connected to personal situations, actions or even thoughts. The connection can be harmless and relatively uncomplicated, as given in the figure (Pic. 3—Connectivity: An Example). This scenario captures the essence of the strange connectivity between a person and his surroundings. It is an example of how people may read fanciful meanings into everyday situations. This also illustrates the tendency of our minds to be influenced by the immediate vicinity instead of being contextual in a larger time and scope. The reference span for decisions is localised and immediate, and, deviates from a larger meaningful context.

Some of the afflicted, because of such 'localisation,' also experience *spatial stimuli.* These are stimuli, unconnected with sentient beings in their vicinity, which rise purely out of reading physical arrangements in the environment. The person may impart an underlying meaning to innocuous arrangements of objects surrounding him. Usually, such individuals experience ease or unease, and read an inner message in these arrangements accordingly. An example of such an influence is when a person comes across a street name and infers it to be a personal message. For example, Mahatma Gandhi Road is seen as chiding the person for being a martyr. Since this form of connectivity links insentient objects and uses them for deriving overlaid messages and direction, they can be termed *spatial influencers*.

We can extend this kind of odd interpretations of the mind into an area where theoretical knowledge remains as sketchy and speculative as it is with the other forms of connectivity discussed. This other form of connectivity is from body reflexes or motor symbolism, which we discussed earlier in Chapter 1 in the Section *Eclectic Esperanto*. Recall LAD (Language Acquisition Device) and UG (Universal Grammar) of Chomsky. We could hazard, some bodily reflexes originate from a kind of corporal blueprint in our species. Body language from this blueprint, most of which is specific to a culture or race, could occur almost automatically in toddlers and adults yet to become aware of their bodies.

A gesture such as flipping the palm in the face of another is one such reflex. The gesture occurs when a participant desires a change of pace in the interaction. Another example involves flicking the thumb against the pointing finger, palm facing inwards. This gesture indicates apathy for the other person, while otherwise appearing interested. Yet another example of a gesture—some people slap their right thigh to indicate an interaction is going as desired, and the left thigh when it is not.

Most interpretations of the cues encountered, have an element of subjectivity. Collectively endorsed interpretations therefore vary from environment to environment, differing among social groups, cultures, geographic areas, languages, etc. Such connectivity could influence decisions, in spite of the fact that it seems irrational. Synchronicity is the 'cherry on top' to the imagination and perception of patterns. Overlaid meanings may trick a person into thinking there is something more to gather from inane events or arrangements. Some may perceive the connectivity as an expression of artistic proportions, others see it as mystical interventions, and yet others as subtle psychosocial signals to be built upon. More examples of inventive meanings among the various possible genres of connectivity attributable to the collective mnemonic are in Table 2 (Examples of Connectivity in Various Genres).

| Connectivity Genre | Example and the Speculated or Derived Meaning |
| --- | --- |
| Tradition | Associating footwear with insult and disrespect |
| Superstition | Believing a sneeze is a bad omen |
| Word Play | Conjuring an alternative meaning (e.g. Paris as 'Pair Is') to help the person act during a deadlocked transaction. Or, extending the word 'umbrella' to mean an overarching protective psychic shroud |
| Synchronicity | Using dream-like associations, *déja vu* or coincidences to make decisions. e.g. seeing personal relevance in the sudden appearance of a cat |
| Spatial Influencers | Deriving personal meaning from innocuous objects. e.g. Seeing a traffic sign-post declaring a road one-way as referring to one's own standing in a matter. Or, seeing the placement of a tuning fork on top of a document as contributing meta-physically to its harmonious appeal |
| Corporal Symbolism | Displaying the palm facing outwards with thumb and fingers outstretched to form a 'Y,' expressing a desire to understand and influence the situation |
| Metaphorical | Perceiving a disembodied criticism even when there is none reflecting a deeper insecurity from early childhood pressures to excel |

Table 2. Examples of Connectivity in Various Genres

The tricky aspect is that several people balance the surrogate sense and deal rationally more often than not. This makes them appear normal, but they tend to succumb to this kind of spurious logic when under stress. Many people that subscribe to such cues could be basing decisions on misinterpreted patterns instead of the rational and real context of the interaction. We cannot explain *why* the mind tends towards such vagueness in its perceptions. Perhaps it is residual from our savage beginnings. The cave dwellers had no need to think beyond immediate time and space. Further, the lack of advanced symbolic tools like language may have caused early humans to rely on bodily cues, while the ability to communicate using symbols was still developing. Such primal tendencies from our past as a species may be inhibiting fresh perspectives in the present as individuals.

The corporal, phonetic and other cues of connectivity, which people experience and impart significance to, initially arise as sub-conscious reflexes. Most such cues appear to have a conjured 'form'. Some people hence believe there is a purpose in them. They cause an underlying psychic reaction, and therefore, one may postulate they exist, even when they are not explicitly acknowledged by all of us. There *are*, in all likelihood, communal forms of such subtle cues, which influence interactions. A particular manifestation could be commonplace in the collective mnemonic of a certain race or culture, while the cue may be totally absent or undetected in a different race or culture. A subscribing group may consciously apply certain collective versions, and also deem this an essential survival skill in the context of the group.

Reflect on the possible consequences of applying this misinterpretation and signalling in groups such as families, cults, corporate boardrooms, or governments. The implications are spine-tingling. Do some people say one thing and do another with impunity because of a symbolic licence from the collective mnemonic? Are they manipulating others through the collective mnemonic? Are such people driving society? These were among Nachiket's fears, brought to a head by his sensitivity.

I argue that a subscribing group, through progressive imitation, has etched such cues in the mnemonic. It continues to pass, such a common (or as put forward, uncommon) understanding of cues down generations. Some people introduce such cues deliberately, to intimidate others in interactions. They seem esoterically aware, and knowledgeable, about the use of this spurious surrogate sense. These 'aware' individuals use and misuse their awareness, as they believe using the cues is the right way to function, despite lack of relevance to the context. Usually, such 'aware' people attempt to adjust the power balance in a relationship using such cues. This is why sensitive individuals, at the receiving end, perceive hostility in the public use of such cues instead of seeing it as just another form of transaction or communication.

Recall, the collective mnemonic is an illiterate side of Nature, with corrupted symbolism. Interpretations of such connectivity could therefore be inventive, speculative and idiosyncratic. Again, some of this inventive speculation is harmless, but some beliefs are detrimental to harmonious living and a civilised outlook. People, egged on by popular superstitions and by uncertainty in the sciences, may ascribe magical or religious explanations for the odd cues, serendipity and coincidences experienced. Many are only able to impute speculative meanings, because the collective mnemonic has an unknown—or at best unconfirmed—basis.

It is paramount to appreciate there will be irrelevance and irrationality in much of what we face. Hence, we must avoid trying to make 'logic' out of every bit of sensory trivia, especially when it provokes hostile or aggressive reactions and behaviour. Some of the more personal manifestations of cues (such as the metaphorical kind) may exist to point each of us to our singular fulfilment, and are to be interpreted positively. For example, when some manifestations or cues ostensibly point us to do harm, we can see in them instead, a metaphor that one is probably being unforgiving deep inside, to oneself or others.

> It is paramount to appreciate there will be irrelevance and irrationality in much of what we face.

As implied at the chapter's outset, the collective mnemonic can be enjoyably progressive when its cues are artistic, pure and nurturing. It is better to be detached and positive in our interpretations and responses when it is not. We need not feel taken aback, or prompted to cause injury to oneself or others. We can let the cues play through in a helpful manner. We can choose to be contextual and not confusingly abstract or harmful. We can get proactive, if not *real*. We'll see how.

## *Section Highlights:*

- Some people ascribe a strange connectivity or meaning to sensory trivia in their environment.
- In addition, 'synchronicity' can mystify some people. Synchronicity is an 'acausal connecting principle' that Carl Jung claimed bridges the dream and the real world.
- An afflicted person could look for dream-like or artificial associations within a localised span of reference (just the immediate moment and locality) instead of a larger context, both in time and relevance.
- This connectivity and overlaid meaning is due to the brain's tendency to fabricate coherence even in the random.
- Random events and arrangements appear to have a quirky, yet meaningful order, particularly when people are sensitive or stressed.
- Some people use the inter-connectedness and symbolic associations to intimidate others. They deliberately apply such dubious cues in transactions.
- A sensitive individual, at the receiving end of such cues, could perceive hostility instead of attempts to communicate, and perhaps spiral into a mental affliction.

- Being aware of the brain's tendency to fit trivial stimuli into a surrogate sense can help us demystify much of our environment.
- We can also get to view any disembodied cues we experience as extended metaphors of early trauma, being presented for us to resolve.

## FROM NUISANCE TO SENSE

A sense of extreme isolation and introversion could cause grandiose delusions of personal power—termed 'psychotic grandiosity' in psychiatry. Psychotic grandiosity is often one of the symptoms of schizophrenia. The term refers to a tendency to become obsessively *self-absorbed*. Among other mind-sets, the misreading of reality described in the earlier section could result in a dangerous kind of misperception. Some acquire an inflated notion of their own importance and ability to influence. Such a person could have an exaggerated sense of ownership of everything around him. For example, the person may feel entitled to claim a random passing car as his own. He could also imagine that he is the prime and central player in *all of existence*. A feeling of being one with everything else may be nice to have if it is positive, filled with joy and yet, not harmful or addictive! Still, more often than not, affected individuals believe they are of Universal importance in a harmful or unproductive fashion. Recall Nachiket's feelings of having special powers. Many similar delusions, such as a belief that one is bestowed with total discretion over others, or that of being a divine dispenser of justice, could even be dangerous.

There are subtler manifestations of this kind of grandiosity also. A person could see an extraordinary ability in himself to affect larger happenings by arranging his immediate environment. For example, acts such as placing his pen over a document, he believes influences events related to that document. An afflicted person carries out such arrangements with an obsessive fervour, and a devious paranoid agenda. The person is likely to believe in a supernatural power to influence—such as having the ability to inflict pain by poking pins in a voodoo doll.

Much of our conditioning in religion and other supporting beliefs in our upbringing, routinely tell us we are divine in order to build up self-esteem. They tell us we are built in the image of God. Or, in some cases, we *are* God. This conditioning may be behind the grandiose thoughts in the afflicted. Many feel short-changed if anything suggests that we are unfinished ideas or constant works-in-progress. We seek a sense of completion and gravitate towards anything that bolsters this belief. Psychotic grandiosity may be a fall out from such beliefs housed in the collective mnemonic. It prompts us deceptively, to feel larger than life.

> Much of our conditioning in religion and other supporting beliefs in our upbringing, routinely tell us we are divine in order to build up self-esteem.

*** ✳ ✳ ✳ ***

The collective mnemonic houses spurious cues as well as a propensity towards the grandiose psychotic displays discussed. When combined with hallucinations and delusions, it could prompt superstitious or irrational behaviour in the afflicted. There could be attempts by some to derive meaning in inane events and arrangements in their vicinity, across the range of various possible genres for connectivity (See Table 2). When trying to derive meaning, many such individuals invariably read the cues outside the normal context. It is almost, but not quite, like seeing omens or portents in ordinary events in the immediate surroundings.

There is no clear explanation on why this happens. Only pseudo-scientific or mystical attempts to set right the uneasiness seem to exist currently. We also lack the wherewithal, in the sciences and human ability, to classify this deeper sensing. All the person experiences in these moments may be unease (or sudden ease) at a possible symbolic pattern, a gesture, a phrase, or physical arrangement. People react, but their reactions defy rational explanations. The danger is, an individual may read hostility or aggression, often mistakenly; and then react in the same manner. Alternatively, some people could just become diffident or unresponsive, as in the case of Nachiket.

$$* * *$$

The crux of contending with the different kinds of connectivity discussed is revealed in Jung's crucial observation regarding synchronicity. Jung's conclusion that such events are 'acausal' is vital. This observation is applicable to all forms of random connectivity. We cannot impart harmful meaning or other hostile 'causal' attributes to the cues resulting from connectivity. We must realise that the several forms of the surrogate sense are manifestations of an illiterate but 'symbolic' nature (the collective mnemonic) mimicking intelligence. In some instances, they may need to be seen as allegorical reminders for us to correct something that has not quite gelled with our inner selves as appropriate.

I postulate that to adopt the surrogate sense literally for decisions is to rely on what is irrational. When one tries to make everything in the environment relevant, one is likely to deviate from the real and rational context. Since the meanings suggested by the collective mnemonic are overlaid derivations with nebulous bases, people are likely to feel inadequate on first becoming aware of such cues. Then again, subscribing individuals who are seemingly *well-versed* in the use of such cues, also run the risk of generating wrong signals when they initiate the cues in interactions. This is, as said earlier, because the meanings derived are generally subjective, or at best, esoteric and restricted to groups.

* * *

How can we manage such a surrogate sense and consequent displays of connectivity by the collective mnemonic? We must first become conscious of such a deviant tendency in others and ourselves. We can then respond rationally to the use or misuse of such factors. It is best to ignore the manifestations, as they tend to throw us off-track from the rational. We don't have to get defensive or carried away in the face of such spurious connectivity by the collective mnemonic. As pointed out repeatedly, we need to remain contextual in our interactions. We should react immediately, and with a rational proactive response, when we are affected by such an odd sense. Otherwise, one may be uneasy; from feeling that one has not done enough, or that one lacks a key skill, or that one has inadequate knowledge.

I would suggest you counter the experiencing of cues mentally using the insights discussed. The next best thing to total avoidance, which may be impossible in some environments, is to be detached. Now that you have explanations on why we end up wrongly perceiving connectivity, you can be detached enough to respond proactively. Collaborating constructively, rather than being aggressive or diffident, is a wise response. We must learn to ignore the surreal or harmful, and keep focused on the context. As understood from extending Jung's interpretation of synchronicity to other forms of connectivity, we should only view the cues as inert signals, and not as innately causative forces. If required, we can respond with a neutralising retort, to counter the event or action that triggered the momentary unease. This is a reassuring rejoinder, which contributes to personal poise.

The four-step response that I advise, if and when you feel dragged into such connectivity are:

1.  COUNTER the cue, when you sense it and cannot ignore it, by doing something frivolous like copying it or performing a superfluous action.

A deliberate departure from the surreal will then annul the cue's unsettling intent or nature. For example, if you feel uneasy because a person flipped his palm in your face, steeple the fingers of your hand into a 'bud' in the direction of the instigator. Use *any* retort: verbal, mental or physical, consciously. This kind of response helps you go on with poise in the interaction, because even as you register the invasive attempt or cue, you are able to grant yourself mentally that you have responded to it.

2. FOCUS on the larger real issue or context, and ignore or negate attempts of those who use such cues to intimidate, confuse or disrupt interactions.

When you are discussing any issue, stick to the context despite distractions such as subliminal asides, disembodied influencers, double-entendres, odd gestures or intimidating posturing. Don't allow such influences to strong-arm or derail your focus on the context.

3. MOVE on in time to new transactions and deliberately get beyond the cues to avoid any harmful or confusing impressions.

This means, stop going back to the cue; take the *learning* it has to offer, then brush it off and leave it in the past. Move on.

4. ADD any new cues you come across to your mental list so you can be better prepared, and a lot more proactive, the next time you come across them.

In conclusion, you can try understanding and interpreting the cues as virtual coaches, and not adversarial manifestations. Like any coach, they can sometimes seem taxing but, with an open mind and a reflective disposition, you can analyse, *befriend* and transact using the cues as helpful aids in communication. You don't have to assume that caving in or battling them, are the only available options.

While all this may seem outlandish, a surprising number tend to be victims or perpetrate such cues and connections. Many use spurious connections for making decisions and influencing outcomes amid uncertainty. In a stressed frame of mind, they may try to read between the lines, or spot unintended meaning in postures and gestures. The stressed person may also mistakenly ascribe hostility to the arrangement of objects around them. In extremely deviant behaviour (read seemingly insane or illogical behaviour), rationality takes a back seat, and interactions are carried out using only a surrogate sense (or nonsense!).

One can easily contest what this chapter states, for its lack of backing by academic research, and, perhaps term it a speculative surmise. Yes, I have drawn these conclusions of mystifying social phenomena only from personal observation. Whether proved factual or merely conjectural, restricted in its scope, my intent is to help others. By providing a broader explanation for the practical quirks, I hope to prevent as many people as possible from spiralling down into a mental affliction. My aim is to ensure that people, to the greatest feasible extent, are better equipped to face some peculiarities they may experience.

Whether one is aware or not, flaws in the collective mnemonic, and consequently its cues, may exist. It could be time to know how to face it. If you sense its manifestations, you have seen such an underlying influencer. If you do not, don't be concerned. They are palpable to some only when under inordinate stress. In ordinary circumstances, we would not sense the manifestations, so don't think you are missing something. If you do have to face them at some point in your life, these sections are an explanation for what you encounter. If it turns out that you also find a better explanation, please adopt it.

Let us now look at yet another way of getting equipped to face the social maelstrom—addressing the third problem pointed out in Part 1—the consequences of civilisation's *virtual scorecard.*

## *Section Highlights:*

- Some afflicted people, display a sense of 'psychotic grandiosity' and believe they have super-human or extra-sensory powers.
- Some could also believe that changing the arrangements of objects in their vicinity, like poking pins into a voodoo doll, can affect remote events.
- Such beliefs are a part of the flawed collective mnemonic, which suggests a hidden order and mystical connections in events that are otherwise inane.
- People could believe there is something more to be learned from the cues when actually, there may be nothing other than the obvious and evident.

- The best way to approach the second problem of flawed cues is to treat them as inert signals, and consciously construct our efforts around the real and meaningful context.
- We need not cave in or respond with hostility, but instead be proactive in countering the cues, moving on and adding any cues we perceive to our experience.

**6**

# DESIRE

'Doctor, I think I know what I have to do,' said Nachiket with new bravado. 'I can talk to people and become involved in politics. I think I can make a difference, and I could even become President if I put my mind to it. That is the way I can make up for lost time and also have people respect me.'

Dharmaraj immediately saw the signs. Nachiket was overreacting to compensate for what he saw as failure. The doctor felt that instead of using plain talk, he had to approach the issue differently. 'I am pleased with your confidence, Nachiket,' he said. 'You can focus on the immediate next steps first. You must relax and get back to having fun with the family, or go back to school, or say… pick up a nice doable hobby.'

Nachiket held up his hands in a frustrated fashion. 'Look at me—how will anybody believe I am normal? I need an accomplishment to wash away my past.'

Dharmaraj quoted once again: 'If your happiness depends on what somebody else does, I guess you do have a problem. You should realise that if success depends wholly on the perceptions of others, you will feel limited, whatever you get to achieve. There will always be a tendency to underplay yourself when you use such a yardstick. What you have experienced is a setback. Learn from it and decide that you are a unique individual whose only mission in life is to get better in some manner, unrelated to any victory over anyone else.'

Nachiket was blustering once again. 'But when I see the achievements of others, I feel small. I feel handicapped. I have been thinking how I can measure up to be a social success.'

'True success is to better yourself every day,' Dharmaraj reassured Nachiket. 'If you find the position of another inspiring, pursue that goal. However, if you do not feel inspired and only inadequate or envious, it may be time to realise that goal is not yours. You have a unique destination. Be patient; you will find your calling as you begin to learn more and more about your capabilities.'

'I have lost so much time. Look at people like Bill Gates. He probably makes a million every few minutes.' Nachiket was having a hard time giving up comparative measures.

'As long as you rely on comparisons for your sense of achievement, all you do will seem insufficient,' the doctor pointed out. 'Why not focus on getting better and better instead?'

'But everything I want to do costs money,' declared Nachiket. 'Nobody cares if you are useful or not, as long as you have money. Don't you think money is a worthwhile goal?'

'Money is important, but it is not everything,' Dharmaraj responded. 'What is more important is to develop faith in your ability to improve, regardless of the situation you are in. There will be a tremendous surge in confidence if you work towards this personal security. Work towards your capability to make money, and not money itself. Money then becomes an automatic consequence of your capability and the value you have to offer.'

'Doctor, people make money without being capable, by unfair and unreasonable means. I have lost a lot of ground. How do I be reasonable and still make money?' said a worried Nachiket.

'You have not lost ground. You have gained insight.' The doctor reminded Nachiket. 'This is more than what several *normal* people can claim. Many people go blindly about their lives and are shocked out of their wits at misfortune. However, you can pre-empt this by having the right intent. You can set the intent to achieve what you want, without having to feel overly affected by the ups and downs in the process. Think about what you are going to do in small steps of achievement, and revel in these. The big ones come to those who have the humility to appreciate the little results. Money is important, but it is a consequence of your focus and cannot be its cause. Your primary need should be absolute betterment. Focus on getting better holistically instead of dwelling on any shortcomings, mental or material. The shortcomings you perceive are, in some sense, locking you in the past.'

'Isn't my past also a lesson?' Nachiket remarked, seeming to catch on to the thin line between dwelling in the past and learning from it.

'Surely!' exclaimed the doctor 'We do not recognise this readily because most of us have not squarely looked at our past. It just happened. We are not able to distance ourselves from the events, and hence we cannot see the lessons.'

'Is there a way to realise these lessons now?' asked Nachiket.

'There is an exercise that would help you to align yourself. It involves writing out the past; looking at it with the perspective that you have gained in the intervening time. Let us discuss this...' The doctor taught Nachiket a practise to help him to come to terms with his past[29].

Dr Dharmaraj was sure he was on the right track. Nachiket had begun to hope, and in real terms. He had become concerned about worldly achievements, even if he was over-reaching. The doctor advised the parents to encourage Nachiket's realistic needs, and to reassure him that everything could be right again. Nachiket also had to understand that there was nothing wrong with taking medication as long as it was necessary. He should treat medication as assistance by modern science to which he need not attach any stigma.

## HAND-BRAKES OFF?

The third issue affecting Nachiket and contributing to his schizophrenic condition was civilisation's virtual scorecard. This comparative record based on social measures, existed in the collective mnemonic before

---

[29]  See GLP2 "The Archived Anxiety" at the end of book under Good Living Practices

we were born. It will continue to exist in it after we are gone. However, the desire to measure up in such social scoring is sometimes misplaced. Such a desire is misplaced when we feel only a compelling victory over others can buttress self-worth. How then can we be purposeful, in a unique personal fashion, in the face of *any* biased social scrutiny or scoring? Dr Dharmaraj posited that an individual can realise a unique personal purpose that is non-relative and enduring. It happens when we consciously manage constraints such as greed, desire and selfishness. Some feel these aid achievements, but they can become mental brakes that kill performance. They can retard sustained effort.

We will explore two specific brakes that are a consequence of keeping social scores, which I see as generally retarding our progress. Although they may be helpful to a degree, for example when used to overcome personal apathy, these brakes seem to trigger a wide range of impairment. They prevent the recognition of an independent personal success. This happened in Nachiket's case. Once we release the brakes, we are more likely to become comfortable with our life's purpose. We develop our own set of standards, deliver our personal best, and appreciate the grace of life.

The first emotional brake we will explore is envy. The harmful thinking that first leads to extreme introspection—and perhaps schizophrenia, or some other dark phase—could have roots in envy or jealousy. Envy is seeded in a false feeling of inadequacy caused by misplaced desires. It may have sentenced some people to feel that they are less than what others are, despite having their own achievements. The envious person feels his achievements cannot measure up to the expectations of the world or his own expectations of himself.

Popular standards in the collective mnemonic at times override our ability to be satisfied with personal achievement. Therefore, capable people become envious too. Adopting comparative standards of success are among the factors that throw regular people into extreme, and sometimes damaging, introspection. The introspection, prompted by desires based on comparisons, can even lead to a mental crisis as happened with Nachiket. We may lack the sense of a distinct self-worth that makes life fulfilling.

> Popular standards in the collective mnemonic at times override our ability to be satisfied with personal achievement.

One cannot appreciate effort or emulate excellence when one is envious. Envy is not a result of disagreement with an idea or event. There could be intellectual and rational understanding that there is merit or popularity in the envied person's success. Still, another person's success may be impossible to accept due to our personal anxieties. The question, the hidden agenda of envy asks, is along the lines of *what does that person have, that I cannot deliver, given the same circumstances and opportunity?* It is difficult to sense personal success if we compare everything we do purely against something others have been successful at. This in fact, is probably, almost everything. Hence, it is important to disconnect our sense of achievement from comparative measures and connect it to inner well-being instead.

Envy can also change in intensity as a reaction to the degree of others' successes. When another person gets a better car, envy might crop up. When this individual gets a second car, this feeling could become more intense, especially when what one has in mind is a similar car. The timing or probability of our getting the car we desire seems unfavourable, triggering a host of harmful feelings. Disturbing feelings may arise from the usual triggers commonly suspected to prompt comparisons, such as high-school reunions, or from less notorious causes, such as advertising propaganda. The question is—why do we compare ourselves to others, and sometimes, end up feeling inadequate? Why is it that we are unable to accept or celebrate the success of those we dislike? That then is the problem. The best way to tackle this is to realise that the other person's achievements have nothing to do with our dreams, except when they are an inspiration.

When is envious desire inspiring and when is it counter-productive? A question that helps add clarity is, 'Does the fulfilment of our desire cater to a necessity or not?' Of course, food, clothing and shelter are necessities. In the early days of humankind, the cave dweller had to kill game to feed his family. Hunting was a necessity, as cultivating crops was unknown. However, there is one thing that sets such killing apart. The basic needs of survival—food, clothing and shelter— required some action, killing animals being one such action. Survival needed it to be performed, which is what separates it from pointless killing. We could make a similar distinction between right and wrong, responsible and irresponsible, appropriate and wishful desires, and other such dichotomies, by realising what is valid for us.

Validation comes from telling *needing* and *wanting* apart. Needing is a rational desire, while wanting, as defined for our discussion, is an irrational one. A 'need' is usually constructive, and cannot be done without. It is a rational desire. A 'want' is usually irrational and generally adds to personal imbalance. A need aligns positively with the axes of nature, individual, and community. A want might compromise one of the axes[30]. Your need is a consuming desire to get something for yourself whereas your want is a consuming desire to get something someone else has, or to deprive someone of something. It could also be a completely irrational obsession. A want is always for something extra, and usually exceeds a person's needs.

Some wants masquerade as needs. Such wants may require fulfilment for they seem to be a prerequisite to our larger goals. For example, a mobile phone is a vital tool to almost everyone. However, my goal of doing business with leading personalities could force me to consider not just *a* mobile phone, but also a top-of-the-line model. Is this a need or a want? Now, what

---

[30]    See section titled 'Severed Stakes'

happens when I am unable to get this phone and a sneaky, no-good, slimy competitor, whom I dislike intensely, already has one? Since we live in society, it is likely that someone would already have what we desire before we get it (assuming we ever do).

When people don't even have what they need, they lack necessities that they defined for themselves. They are not self-sufficient. They are trying to fill in something missing, without which they feel their life is incomplete. It is part of their dream and vision. So, is the desire for a top-of-the-line model cell phone a need or a want? Is Nachiket's desire to be President a need or a want? Questions of this kind can be answered only with a personal perspective and assimilating the following explanation.

We can see our desires in the right light by considering a statement and some concepts based on the

> 'We can get anything we need, but we cannot get everything we want.'

*Life 101* series by John-Rogers (aka Roger D Hinkins)[31] and Peter McWilliams (1949–2000)[32]. They coined the phrase, 'We can get anything we want, but we cannot get everything we want.' Reword that to—'We can get anything we need, but we cannot get everything we want[33].' The unusual realisation from this is that we must accept an 'unworthiness' (Yes, unworthiness!)

---

[31] Roger Delano Hinkins, known and published as John-Rogers, is an American author and public speaker

[32] Peter Alexander McWilliams was an American self-help author

[33] McWilliams, Peter: *Do It! Let's Get Off Our Buts*. Atlantic Books, 1998.

which allows us to do without anything that is not earmarked as ours. Unworthiness is a realisation that some things are not structured to come to us, with and without effort. Believe me; this unworthiness is supportive if we unlink the semantic baggage the word normally carries. Indoctrination by social standards of success, many of which are housed in the collective mnemonic, can prevent us from accepting this. Our ego refuses unworthiness due to its perceived connotations. It gives rise to feelings of being psychologically small. Nevertheless, when we see it as a guiding force, taking us towards our own singular fulfilment, we will feel comfortable with it.

We have to view this unworthiness as a friend, just as we do worthiness. These two feelings keep us on the path to what is truly ours—our own dreams and not somebody else's. Unworthiness is the friend that says, 'Your proper path is not this way.' Unworthiness is not a disconnection with our purpose, but a compass indicating the path to our own specific success. The sense of not being on track (being unworthy) leads to discovering what you can enjoy and accomplish (what you are worthy of).

Dr Dharmaraj, in his dialogues, was trying to transform the confused feelings of worthiness and unworthiness that Nachiket was experiencing into a constructive and usable force. I believe, we misinterpret unworthiness and express it as envy. If whatever is envied is truly our path, we would feel somewhat inspired, not abrasive and envious. Whether we consider the envied person deserving or not does not matter. The result inspires us. If there is only envy without inspiration, then that may not be a true goal. Attaching aspirations to some independent dimension, de-linked from the envied entity, would release a tremendous amount of energy for effort, and hence, a separate success. The key is to channel the ability to appreciate another's success into a capability to be aware of our own pluses.

We lose control if we tie up our own deep-set goals with the achievements of others and keep score. Instead of feeling a sense of ownership to our own goals, desires, and needs,

> We lose control if we tie up our own deep-set goals with the achievements of others, and keep score.

we try to imitate or compare ourselves with others. Naturally, several of us would then feel out-of-control, or experience misaligned emotions. We are always reacting to someone else's standing, instead of being proactive and influencing our own. We need to realise we are not doing what we do just to be better than someone else. We do what we do to better our own concerns. With this realisation, we can remain unaffected by the *taunting* of others, and the *flaunting* of their achievements. When we grant the fact, each of us is free to live our own independent lives; we will no longer have desires conditioned by others. With this mind-set, we can easily validate desires and funnel them into driving those energies that help us function and achieve our best, *without keeping score*. We develop the capacity to appreciate our own achievements and those of others without resorting to comparisons. And... even as we appreciate, we aspire to acquire only what inspires!

We had a look at desire and its ramifications on an emotional plane in this section. We will look at the physical plane, that of wealth and luxury, in the next.

<u>*Section Highlights:*</u>
- The primary repercussions of society's virtual scorecard are those of being envious of others, and/or being dissatisfied with what we possess.
- We can ascertain the validity of our goals and desires by classifying them into rational needs or irrational wants.
- For our discussions, fulfilment of a need typically does not upset anyone including oneself, but fulfilling a want is likely to disturb others, or, result in an imbalanced self.
- When a desire or a dream is disconnected from inspiration and is based instead on comparisons, it can be a brake on effective functioning and progress.
- When we recognise 'unworthiness' as a blessing that approves us to not have that which does not belong to us, we get clarity on the things we need and are 'worthy' of.

## THE WORRY OF WEALTH

Another inhibition resulting from the collective mnemonic's *virtual scorecard* is the worry arising from incorrect attitudes towards wealth. They can impact an individual and force the feelings of inadequacy, causing unease and schizoid reactions. How can we become comfortable with wealth and how much of it we have?

Effort may only be one of the ingredients necessary to acquire a *sense* of wealth. Some put in enormous effort and still feel poor. Yet others acquire great wealth with what seems like little effort. Such contradictions plagued Nachiket because his attitude towards wealth, like several others, was mixed-up. A burning desire for wealth causes confusion. There is a feeling of inadequacy with whatever wealth one already has, and an obsessive incessant craving to possess more and more. Let me propose an alternative explanation on how we can be personally wealthy and confident, whatever be the quantum of surplus or perceived deficit in wealth.

Despite the social temptations, which prompt us to treat wealth as a benchmark of success, you have it in you to enjoy the coffee and disregard the cup. This statement is based on a modern-day parable that was doing the rounds on the internet, and goes as follows: A group of alumni, well established in their careers, got together to visit their old University professor. Conversation soon turned into complaints about stress in work and life. Offering his guests coffee, the professor went to the kitchen and returned with a large pot and an assortment of cups—porcelain, plastic, glass, and crystal—some plain looking, some expensive, some exquisite—telling them to help themselves to hot coffee.

When all the students had a cup of coffee in hand, the professor said, 'If you notice, all the nice-looking expensive cups were taken up, leaving behind the plain and cheap ones. While it is but normal for you to want only the best for yourselves: *that* is the source of your stress. What all of you really wanted was coffee, not the cup—but you consciously went for the best cups and were eyeing each other's cups. Now if life is coffee, then the jobs, money, and position in society are the cups. They are just tools to hold and contain life. Sometimes, by concentrating only on the cup, people fail to enjoy the coffee in it.'

Let me begin with an attempt at annulling the common uneasiness that the distribution of wealth in society is unjust and uneven. To this end, consider that longing for

> There must never be a satisfying amount or distribution of wealth in society, if the capital markets are to sustain.

wealth could be a necessary lubricant for the civilisation machine. Perhaps, we need some people to be dissatisfied with whatever wealth they have. Those dissatisfied with their wealth and occupied with wealth creation keep the markets churning. There must never be a satisfying amount or distribution of wealth in society, if the capital markets are to sustain. No one would risk investment if all were secure in their quantum of wealth. A person who flogs his horse of wealth due to dissatisfaction could be in a symbiotic relationship with those who find satisfaction in value creation. Can anything get better in the real sense without increasing in value? We can desire wealth, but it is not advisable to have an obsession to measure ourselves with wealth alone as a score, ignoring or giving lesser importance to value. We can make a better choice by keeping wealth subservient to the aim of holistic personal betterment and progress. Enjoy the value you create, rejoice in betterment, and make wealth a consequence, not the cause.

Wealth inspires value. On the flip side, value inspires wealth as well. For money to avoid the ills of stagnation, it needs to flow in society. Therefore, imbalances may be a natural way to keep it flowing. Just as we obtain electricity through the flow of water, it is the flow of money that allows us to tap its power—the power of value. Imbalanced wealth is the engine of growth. In fact, creating money *with* money is the new industry of this age, and a recognised and respected profession. We have come a long way from attributing money-lending to Shylocks and sharks. Both value for money and money for money are aspects of value creation. We need players in the money game and the producers of other measurable 'value' in a beneficial two-way relationship.

Is that all? NO! There is yet another class of confusion related to wealth. Consider the confusion caused by looking at wealth as an approval mechanism. This is different from the unease caused by a craving to get the greatest quantum of wealth possible. Some historical standards endorse the mistaken notion that wealth will garner approval. This is again a problem created by popular yardsticks of success housed in the collective mnemonic. There is a lot out there to mislead us too. Nachiket appears confused as well. He misinterpreted wealth and saw it as a mechanism to garner approval.

Wealth is usually a consequence of the value offered being approved. But some feel instead that approval can be bought by wealth. A person could seek approval, and look for it by increasing his wealth and possessions. He does not see the benefits he can reap from the approval of his value creation. The kind of approval invited using wealth alone as a measure, is usually sycophancy.

A conviction that approval is because of wealth comes from a lack of personal security and a lack of faith in oneself and Creation. When we adopt a comparative yardstick (especially wealth) to measure self-esteem and personal success, there will always be a sense of failure. All the steps we take, even when in the right direction, will defy a sense of accomplishment when we base it on comparative and shifting yardsticks of wealth. The more a person tries for closure using only wealth as a measure, the more inadequate it will seem to be. The proverbial pot of gold at the end of the rainbow is impossible to reach, and does not exist. When one measures rewards differently, one would see wealth as a secondary benefit, and not a primary goal.

The issue that makes people adopt comparative standards of wealth, in spite of life meeting their needs, is the constant parade of so-called better lifestyles. Again, as

> If we reach beyond our capability for pleasure, without a proper attitude towards it, such pleasurable experiences may tantalise and leave us frustrated.

already discussed, there are media and marketing wizards touting the great pleasures that wealth will confer upon us. However, pleasure is perhaps a one-way street. If we experience a higher form of pleasure, it is unlikely that the lesser forms will be adequate after that experience. If we reach beyond our capability for pleasure, without a proper attitude towards it, such pleasurable experiences may tantalise and leave us frustrated.

Needless to add, there is always that unbelievable holiday in the magnificent home of your schoolmate, or the extravagant outing which your wealthy uncle sponsored; or that lavish gourmet dinner your boss took you out to, or the texture of your neighbour's expensive designer dress brushing against you, or even that incredible electronic gizmo, which your kid played with at his friend's house, about which *your* kid gets dreamy eyed… The list of serendipitous pleasures we may come across is endless, restricted only by our imagination.

What kind of fate allows people to glimpse pleasure that is clearly outside of today's menu, i.e. out-of-reach pleasures that we experienced by pure chance? How can we cherish and not get wistful about such experiences? Here is where the individual needs to make the decision whether a form of pleasure is a personal goal or not. Our goals for accomplishment and pleasure have to be in consonance with larger, yet realistic personal needs. If it is realistic and not fanciful, we can make such goals and desires part of our personal purpose. It is a *need*.

We also ought to make a decision that having a need has nothing to do with enjoying our todays. Obsession destroys the moment. What is the difference between a person craving a drug fix and a person craving a form of acceptable pleasure? Fundamentally nothing, if one is uneasy without them. We need not destroy the moment by obsessing over something that is not remotely attainable in the palpable future. From today, let your capability in the present, and the feasible capabilities in the future, drive you to the pleasures of *your* life. Can a shot of an intoxicant enduringly resolve our problems? Can a custom-made perfume at $65,000 an ounce really solve a self-esteem problem? I think not. We can build a durable self-image only by having absolute cornerstones.

You have seen several people putting in more than a reasonable measure of effort for personal wealth and the glamour attached to it. Some harried executives, constantly travelling show-biz personalities, and the occasional ulcerated CEO would fit this description very well. The extent of unease, mental and physical, that some are willing to go through for the sake of wealth is sometimes unimaginable. The answer, to the question of why they do it, could be fear of losing their lifestyle, or fear of losing parity and favour with *peers*. They are afraid to say, 'Enough.' They fear that at some point, enough may not be enough. They are also among those who swing on the scales of comparative worth and cannot get off.

Despite having said all that, we must also appreciate that there are many who invest great effort in the acquisition or maintenance of wealth because they have found larger concerns. They do not focus just on personal wealth for motivation. They are the value-creators, and wealth to them is a consequence of being socially active. Wealth to them is a means to a greater holistic end. They connect its acquisition to what they believe to be the greater good. Results from such an objective are usually constructive and in harmony with improving self, our society and the natural environment.

We may need a shift in attitude to acquire true comfort with our monetary goals and status. We can deliver value and excellence, and get better holistically, when our world does not solely revolve around wealth, and its scoring in comparison to others. The doctor was trying to make Nachiket see that chasing ever-increasing wealth need not result in increasing security or satisfaction. The answer is to expand your goal to get better in all aspects, and not just wealth. 'The pursuit of happiness' is not the same as the pursuit of wealth. We would get better—and consequently, even wealthier—because we are inherently enterprising and focused on creating value.

An abundance mentality leads to abundance. Expect that you will always have money and you will have it. Uneasiness with money leads to inappropriate drives and action in the management of wealth. Imagine those who are uncomfortable with money. The minute they have more, they get a feeling that things are abnormal. Such people go and spend irrationally, just to ease the discomfort or worry of having wealth. If instead, we like to have money, money will stay with us. Perhaps the key to real wealth is to like it. Of course, this does not mean hoarding money, but being comfortable with it. We should not find money sinful, wasteful, or unjust. When we become comfortable with money, we discover wealth.

✻ ✻ ✻

I hope that this discussion puts to rest any frustrating search to acquire the greatest quantum of wealth we can have, and any frustration with the distribution of wealth in society. While we can support the 'have-nots' in regard to their needs, we need not compare the quantum of wealth with the 'haves'. We need to annul questions such as, *How are some people 'wealthy' without contributing value? Why is wealth, as commonly measured, an acceptable yardstick of success?* and *When is wealth enough?* Such questions are unnecessary and without significance. Go beyond them. Look instead for ways to contribute value.

Wealth is not for approval. Wealth is not purely to make living pleasurable. Wealth comes through value, not the other way around. *Enough* and *more*, after a certain threshold, are states of mind, not states of the material. Whatever you feel currently—as a have or a have not—you can get better and successful if your personal outlook towards wealth is a sincere invitation. With patience, we can sow, and we can reap. When you welcome personal success, the floodgates of *reward* will open, sure enough. As Louise Hay, the author of *You Can Heal Your Life* says—'If the Universe has provided you with enough air to last you till your last breath—is it not possible to have faith in it, that the rest will also be provided?'

The ultimate sense of security should be from your own existence, its learning, and betterment. Twists and turns in fate can bring or take away material wealth. However, if you groom yourself, day by day, to do, learn and enjoy in life…that is true wealth. Try ignoring the circumstances you are in now and ask yourself—*Have I learnt my lessons, and am I better equipped to deal with life today than I was a year ago?* The answer, for most of us, is likely to be an emphatic 'YES!'

When we value our growth and our ability to be proactive, whatever the circumstances, we come to appreciate the present and keep hopeful for the time to come. We are not condemned to any bittersweet nostalgia, and learn to thrive in the present and plan for the future. We cherish our reality, and have the will and the patience to turn things around if required. Accept today—tough, as it may seem. Keep feeling, volitionally, that there is a beneficial change being affected, somewhere…someplace. Keep growth, learning and maturity as your measures of wealth. Strangely, we will feel wealthy only when we discover this, whether you have no money, a few dollars, or, millions in surplus.

✳ ✳ ✳

In this Part, we saw how to view the three problems pointed out in Part I. Now, not all people view popular standards on winning, the collective cues, and desires to be superior as stifling. Despite the heavy mental load they impose, several bear them willingly in the hope that one day they will prevail. This is the lure of the mirage. It will be deflating to have this pointed out. Unless we replace this mirage with something real, it may sap motivation. An initial understanding of the concept of personal purpose serves as an alternative motivating factor. It can anchor each of us in our unique betterment.

A unique personal purpose is really an individual's discovery over time and may require patience. Hence, some would be sceptical until the revelation of their purpose. Part IV is an attempt to remove any last shreds of doubt on the benefits of acquiring a reasonable personal purpose. It attempts to explain: why conflict, why differences, why challenges, why reason, and, why this Creation. In Part IV are more explanations for several such 'whys' in our minds.

The friends and foes in our history leave deep impressions on us. We are agitated and driven to some things because of harmful events in the past. Flawed experiences may overly influence our decisions today. Our past could contain events that stop us from breaking free and coming to the present. The impacts of such events on the psyche have to be managed. It is imperative that we come to terms with our past if we are to have a reasonable outlook. This brings up the next GLP to explore—*The Archived Anxiety*, a potent technique.

## *Section Highlights:*

- Uneven distribution of wealth, and a desire to possess more, may be social mechanisms that ensure continued investment in value creation.
- Wealth is a consequence of approval, and not a cause. One cannot 'buy' genuine approval.
- *Enough* and *more*, after a certain basic threshold, are a state of the mind, not the material.
- We can cherish the out-of-reach chance pleasures we experience, but we also need to enjoy the moment and be comfortable, even in their absence.

- A misplaced sense of dearth could prompt unreasonable behaviour or deny us the recognition of our personal purpose.
- The sense of being wealthy comes from a gradual development of an unshakeable confidence to 'gain' in any environment.
- If we are comfortable with wealth, and our personal ability to feel confident and effective, we are rewarded in both the material and mental aspects.
- A mentality of abundance will lead to greater palpable abundance in many facets of life.

# PART IV: The Confirmation

*What's it all about? Why are we here? What's the point? Is there a point? Why bother?*

*Why life?*

At some point, you have probably pondered The Meaning of Life, and you came up with a satisfactory answer, which has, or has not, stood the test of time. Or you shrugged mightily, muttered, 'Beats the hell out of me', and ordered another cheeseburger. *The Meaning of Life*. Very funny; very true.

The question that precedes 'What's the meaning of life?' is of course, '*Is there* a meaning to life?' Beats the hell out of me (again). I'm going to explore the first question as though the answer to the second question is yes.

If it's true that life has no meaning, no purpose then it doesn't matter whether I've consumed a few pages speculating on it. So let's play a game called Life Matters.

We'll start the game by *assuming* there is a purpose. The first question of Life Matters: What is the purpose of life?

Here's my answer:

Life is for doing, learning, and enjoying.

—Peter McWilliams (1949–2000),
*Life 101* Series

# DIVERSITY

'Dr Dharmaraj, I am beginning to think a lot more clearly, more often than before. I can actually direct my flow of thoughts and focus better. Does this mean I am forgetting the learning I thought I had from my past?' asked Nachiket.

'Nachiket, every mind is remarkable. The sooner you acknowledge that your thoughts are yours alone, the sooner you will be able to reap the benefits, past and present,' the doctor replied matter-of-factly.

'The more I write, the more I am convinced that "I" want to be heard for what I am today, and not as some spokesperson from another life,' Nachiket said firmly.

'You have just begun to discover yourself as a unique individual, as a person who can make choices,' Dharmaraj said, barely hiding his delight at the progress Nachiket was making. 'It is, in a way, the awakening we discussed. You will find your chosen agreements and differences from the moment you acknowledge that you can be in control.'

'But disagreement is conflict,' Nachiket observed. 'I had no doubts earlier, right or wrong! I wonder if I was more focused before.'

'No, Nachiket. Your clarity has changed from a small to a large and more absolute perspective,' said Dharmaraj. 'Perhaps the fear of standing up and disagreeing where you should, holds you back. Just imagine…if we all agreed to one side of the story, what a lopsided world we would live in. It is important to disagree, because in disagreements lie personal and political freedoms.'

'Are you saying there is no universal truth on which we all can agree?' quizzed Nachiket.

The doctor spoke carefully. 'Assume there is such a thing momentarily, but consider that the human mind is limited in its ability to understand it. Hence, we have to choose, in our limited fashion, a facet of the truth…while several facets may seem valid. We may or may not ever agree as a race,' said Dharmaraj, 'but unless we disagree we will not go towards what may be a universal truth. We solve complexities, sort out disagreements, and get lifted to higher and higher planes of understanding.'

'Why should the Creator want this? That we should fight and disagree? Why not simply reveal the truth?' asked Nachiket.

'To paraphrase from a movie… Can you handle the truth?' said Dharmaraj with a pause. 'Imagine a limitless universe stretching way beyond our senses. Is it not good that our existence reveals it one moment at a time, one portion at a time, for us to fully experience? A limitless Universe we know exists, but we do not let it come in the way of our day-to-day life. The truth is your existence will allow you to experience it a little at a time.'

'In other words,' Nachiket remarked, 'I was created with some limitations so that I can experience the limitless from some standpoint.'

'An insightful observation… for if we were limitless, there would be no measurable experience!' exclaimed the doctor.

'But not everyone has the same limitations,' continued Nachiket. 'What to me is crystal clear may not be clear to someone else. This can cause conflict.'

'Yes,' agreed the doctor. 'To recognise the truth that is common to all, we may have to go through several iterations. It all becomes a lot clearer with just the passing of time and the keeping of an open mind. If you still have conflict, then it is your chosen disagreement.'

'Then conflict is inevitable…?' posed Nachiket.

'Yes and no,' the doctor said slowly. 'You may have external conflict, but you do not have conflict within yourself once you think through your chosen disagreement. It could also be true that disagreements are the way creation keeps its balance…'

'… or even provides the energy for its continued pulsing as it rocks back and forth?' said Nachiket, getting imaginative.

'Possibly,' conceded the doctor. 'It would be pretty hard to get any movement or variety without attraction and repulsion. This would be the case in an existence where everything was uniform.'

'I am beginning to understand conflict when I take the words you say and add to it what I have learned from various scriptures,' said Nachiket, pensively.

'And what is that?' asked the doctor.

'From the scriptures, we know that despite conflict, there is a chosen duty, an altar for action. I think there is a personal answer in that,' reflected Nachiket.

'Nachiket, do take your medicines regularly. It will help you focus. Do you still hear voices?' inquired Dharmaraj.

'No… I feel as if I have brought my existence back within my body,' said Nachiket, smiling. 'The sound is just a mumble. I cannot make out what is being said even if I try hard.'

'Good! Good!' said the doctor. Clearly, the hallucinations were receding. 'Transcend any residual hallucinatory triggers by either trying to learn from them, or by ignoring them. Here is a tip: Distract yourself by doing some easy reading or listening to music. Have you been writing down your history as I suggested?'

'Yes, I have, but there are some memories that won't leave me,' Nachiket confessed, stating a problem anybody could have. 'Some mistakes I have made haunt me.'

'Let's explore a way of handling these disturbing memories,' said the doctor, launching into another technique[34].

Real memories were now the basis for Nachiket's insecurities. Such fears were *normal*. If Nachiket kept

---

[34]    See GLP3 "Forgive to Forget" at the end of the book under Good Living Practices

up with his medication as long as it was necessary, the likelihood of a relapse was remote. He needed to interact with others and realise that life did not challenge him alone—that life and its challenges were for everyone. Nachiket needed to know that he could have a point of view, regardless of conflicting opinions. He needed to realise that universal agreement or equilibrium is a perpetual work in progress.

## DEFUSING DICTATORSHIP

One cannot exorcise the *disorienters* in the collective mnemonic completely. Many disorienting influences are deep-set. Some are quite obviously conflicting and compound the confusion experienced by a patient of schizophrenia. We see many differences in practices and beliefs, hence, doubts can crop up. We often harbour questions regarding our journey through life. Why does it seem as if there are several valid orientations for personal purpose in the first place? Why are there diverse rules and philosophies? Why so much difference in opinions on right and wrong? What justifies these different beliefs in creation, and sometimes the need to fight for what we believe? Questions like these triggered Nachiket's core unease, and led to the larger disorder. Nachiket was uneasy as he felt there should be no external conflict before he could choose what to do. The reason for this, again,

> Several social, religious, and political ideologies in the collective mnemonic are misleading in their promise of a single Universal Law.

could be the collective mnemonic. It has conflicting ideas, but also houses a belief that there is some single universal truth, with which all conflict can be overcome. Several social, religious, and political ideologies in the collective mnemonic are misleading in their promise of a single Universal Law.

Dharmaraj suggested leaving the grandiose thoughts of an all-encompassing all-pervading unity for a while, since it can distract one from understanding a personal purpose, and our path to betterment. I postulate that we need to recognise that different points of view are necessary for the effective functioning of humankind. People need to disagree. When we experience conflict, this only moves disagreements to a higher plane. On such a plane, there is greater learning, and our choices become more evident.

Consider the continuing argument on whether industry should be controlled by the government or just follow the principle of unbridled *laissez-faire*. Regardless of the growing global village, we cannot compromise the sovereignty of a country to accommodate corporate balance sheets. On the flip side, a country is not sovereign because of its bureaucracy. Industry and State have to be independent, and act to balance the profit motive with fair practices. An industrialist cannot be an administrator of laws, and the State is not a business. Hopefully, these camps will always be distinct.

What about the doctrines of vegetarianism and meat-eating? Arguing for vegetarians, sourcing of meat is mostly barbaric and painful. Arguing for meat-eaters, what one eats may not measure our compassion. Mother Teresa apparently ate meat, and Hitler apparently was a *flexitarian*[35]. Some research also claims that vegetarians have a higher likelihood of poor mental health from not ingesting meat that has natural Omega-3 fatty acids. Then, there is the naïve question *Will our ecosystem remain balanced if the entire world turns vegetarian?* On the other hand, isn't taking the life of animals just a gateway to taking the life of a higher life form? If we agree with one side of this issue, it is important to disagree with the other to ensure continued balance. In this argument on being a vegetarian or a meat-eater, we can belong to one or the other camp; even debate it, but reserve passing judgements on a person who has made a different choice. Bottom line is that as a species, we *are* omnivores, as evidenced by the way our dentures have evolved. Our tastes may differ within this definition as well.

Another continuing debate is the one over aggressive advertising and our right to privacy. An icon of advertising, Neil French, anonymously advertises a non-existent beer. Soon people are asking vehemently for the beer[36]. He presumably, could sell the brand to a manufacturer *without a product in place*. Early advertising objectively informed the public of the availability of a product or service. It did not overtly influence the buying decision. Advertising has changed greatly since then. Nobel laureate in Literature, Aleksandr Solzhenitsyn (1918-2008), was prompted

---

[35] "Flexitarian" is a recent term coined to describe one whose diet is normally meatless but occasionally includes meat or fish. See http://www.merriam-webster.com/dictionary/flexitarian

[36] This was done by him to collect data on the impact of Print as a medium compared to other emergent media

by the proliferation of billboards to comment that it is a 'licence to spit in the eye and soul of the passers-by.' Accepting the important role advertising plays in keeping our news and entertainment within reach of our wallet, governments may still need to regulate and prevent irresponsible invasive advertising.

Dr Dharmaraj was trying to clarify, through reasoning, as I have tried with the foregoing examples, that personal purpose is not a one-point programme. Your personal purpose would accept different points of view, and yet have a clear personal choice within it. When propaganda forces people to think alike, we may as well be heading towards a dictatorship or a terrorist group or a cult. How can we ensure a conceptually brilliant, but paranoid propaganda, such as that of an extreme social order does not enslave us? It seems important that people think differently, *regardless of what appears to be right or wrong.*

✳ ✳ ✳

The preceding examples of opposing viewpoints may seem contrived, but they demonstrate why it is important to disagree. It is best that some issues remain unresolved. See-sawing conflicts are the bases of individual sovereignty. By disagreeing, people prevent the frightening scenario of authoritarian powerful points of control as depicted in George Orwell's fiction. Perhaps this is why the collective mnemonic exists in the first place. You are most welcome to disagree with such an idea. In fact, it is best we all agree to disagree for eternity. We should agree, nevertheless, within our own selves. Our integration carries us towards our chosen agreement or disagreement with a focus that translates into successful action.

In a Hindu fable, a sparrow being chased by a hawk takes refuge in the arms of Emperor Sibi. Emperor Sibi was known for his just decisions and compassion. The king of the lesser gods, Indra as the sparrow, and Agni, the god of Fire, as the hawk—were testing him. The sparrow claimed protecting him was the duty of the emperor while the hawk claimed Sibi was denying him his natural prey and food. At this, Sibi offered an equal amount of his own flesh as food for the hawk as an alternative. The two gods then revealed themselves and showered their blessings on Sibi. It seems to me that in our chosen agreements or disagreements we play out a larger personal purpose. Disagreements, when correctly directed, rise to higher planes of relevance, making our personal choices clearer. There is no getting away from a loftier personal choice when we are at a difficult crossroad.

> Disagreements, when correctly directed, rise to higher planes of relevance, making our personal choices  clearer.

Why do people disagree? It is obvious that people can choose differently and think differently. The question is why does one person need persuading when another sees the same claim as a common truth? No doubt, we have different backgrounds, but why doesn't the intellect's reasoning ability bring people together? Why is a universal truth not enthroned? Why do several points of view and versions exist? Are people designed to disagree? For answers, let's look at that part of our physiology that houses our thinking, our brain.

*Section Highlights:*

- Disagreements need to exist in society for checks and balances to be in place.
- When we do away with petty disagreements caused by envy, greed, wealth, power and the like, core issues are what remain.
- Genuine differences keep cults, despots and Orwellian nightmares away. They prevent monopolistic forces and isolating points of view from taking hold.
- There may be an in-built need for people to disagree so that better alternatives can emerge from such a churning.

## DISAGREEMENT BY DESIGN

Scientists have reached some conclusions from the well-known split-brain research. Surgeons severed the connections between the left and right hemispheres of the brain for some patients whose medical condition seemed to warrant such a surgery. When researchers showed an image of an object to the left-brain of these patients, the patients could name it. However, when they showed the same image to the right-brain, the subjects could only pick out a similar object by feeling it. They could not name the object, but they could sometimes articulate its use. It became clear that the left-brain is responsible for symbolic communication (verbal) and the right-brain for understanding relationships in time and space (spatial). It is unimportant whether the mapping based on this study of the brain is accurate or not. At least one study indicates that the feminine left-brain has the capability to share both spatial and verbal features[37]. What is more relevant is the distinct verbal and spatial orientation the brain adopts. It means we have at least two decision-making structures within us that cooperate to make us whole.

Although the collective mnemonic straddles symbolism and instincts (see earlier figure Pic. 1), its impact, both valid and flawed, manifest primarily as a reflex. We sometimes react instinctively without prior reasoning because of strong influences from it. The collective mnemonic juggles the learning of both halves of the brain and this can sometimes be confusing. Our cognitive left portion of the brain typically, attempts to understand using ordered patterns: lingual and symbolic. But, the left-brain is sometimes swayed by speculative right-brain inferences. That is, the 'verbal' left portion of the brain may process spatial arrangements, which are normally in the domain of the right brain, and derive the spurious symbolic patterns discussed earlier. Additionally, researchers' mapping of the brain links the hind-brain to the senses and the fore-brain to motion. Adding more complexity is the fact that the right half of the brain controls the motor actions of the left side of the body and vice versa. Are

---

[37] A study by Shaywitz, Bennet & Sally, reported in the *New York Times,* Feb 16th 1995

these factors relating to the design and functioning of the brain causing confusion in us? Is this why we do not agree as a race?

I argue that our brain sometimes delivers mixed signals, because it functions using diverse physiological locations and numerous criss-crossing neural networks. Random thoughts crop up during discussions of important issues, leading decisions astray. A misplaced emotion or an awkward gesture intrudes into the smooth flow of a conversation. Sometimes a craving engulfs us at an unsuitable moment. We may sporadically experience some spurious cues of the collective mnemonic, as well. Even *déja vu* is hypothesised to occur because of external stimuli being received by the *memory location* in the brain, a fraction before the awareness or *conscious portion* of the brain. This reversed timing in the receipt of stimulus leads to the person feeling he has seen what is perceived before. All of these could interrupt the understanding of one person by another during any interaction. The brain's signals can be confusing. Its design perhaps innately causes disagreements.

Popular thought proclaims that there is a single universal truth or destination out there for us to achieve. This causes many schizophrenia patients to vehemently look for an all-encompassing, zero conflict state. In reality, disagreement may really be the normal state. Perhaps the design of our brain is skewed towards disagreement, and not a single idea. The brain's inherent design of differing locations for action and reaction means that at any point in time, a thought can take many directions within the brain's structure. The brain can reach a wide, and potentially bewildering, array of conclusions as a thinking tool. It is no surprise that different people use this tool in varied ways to reach different conclusions. Incompatible beliefs arose inevitably, across different societies and languages. Consequently, differences in human thought continue. These beliefs cannot—and perhaps should not—coalesce. This means we need not, and cannot agree with everything out there. We can agree or disagree according to our personal choice, and yet look objectively at other choices.

> The brain's inherent design of differing locations for action and reaction means that at any point in time, a thought can take many directions within the brain's structure.

Who knows? Perhaps the way we are physiologically designed and evolved makes human disagreement, and perpetual conflict, a normal state. The social purpose of disagreement is clear, though people find it unpleasant, as suggested from the sampling of opposites in the previous section. Has some force, divine or mundane, designed us to disagree so that we can discover what our personal disagreement should be? Perhaps it is because of this churning and sifting that the intellect of our species developed rapidly. Perhaps this intellectual development is nature's way of knocking sense into the species. Perhaps this is part of the engine of evolution. This design may exist so that we overcome a need to persuade others to follow any isolated belief. It may exist for us to recognise that there is a need for diversity.

Isolating propaganda, poetry or passion that makes for warring factions in us, will not sweep us off our feet when we have a constructive intent that supports diversity. Given that the development of our beliefs as a civilised race were geographically isolated, linguistically distinct, ideologically opinionated and instinctively territorial, disagreement may just be our new normal. We can admit different constructive beliefs or understanding, though we are not in agreement with some (or all) of their tenets. While we disagree, we can respect other progressive understandings, even while campaigning for our own cause. We can validate, accept and honour any different ideology, as long as it is constructive and humane. We *can* disagree, and yet, live and let live.

> While we disagree, we can respect other progressive understandings, even while campaigning for our own cause.

✳ ✳ ✳

Before we go further, consider the possibility that one could have acted unwisely in the past, causing unrest in the present. In the early years, we might have steamrolled others, or sometimes disagreed with our own conscience. Some of our actions may be in stark dissonance with commonly accepted norms, leading to regret or guilt. Our willingness to discover a personal purpose may be hampered by emotional hang-ups from the past. The next GLP is for addressing those acts we regret now, but justified cleverly in the past. To put the memories that haunt us to rest and become self-anchored in our outlook, consider the next GLP, 'Forgive to Forget,' in the Good Living Practices section.

## *Section Highlights:*

- The roots of much conflict may be in a flawed belief that there is a single goal that transcends all disagreement.
- The trait of disagreement, on the contrary, could be hardwired in the human brain's structure and a normal state for us as a species.
- Disagreement and conflict may be evolutionary mechanisms for the human intellect, and inherent in our nature.
- Ideological disagreements, deadlocks, and other impediments to being civilised, are often resolved with wider understanding and constructive *personal* choices.
- When any debate or conflict is genuine, reasonable and humane, it contributes towards us becoming more civilised as a race, regardless of the sides we choose.

# 8

# REASONABLENESS

'I want justice, Dr Dharmaraj. Why did I have this experience? Why me?' Nachiket's pent-up frustrations were coming to a head, and he was having a fit of self-righteousness. His progress and well-being seemed at stake.

Dr Dharmaraj attempted to convert Nachiket's indignation to motivation. 'We cannot always choose what life hands out to us. The positive thing from the whole experience is you can now take a good, objective look at yourself. As I said before, this is more than what some normal people get to do in their entire lives. Most of us float along, going where the tides take us. But no! You sense your current circumstance and perceive a need to do something. This is actually good, Nachiket.'

'My mind is filled with ideas to take short cuts. I want to be on a social par with those who are about my age, and I am willing to do anything…even bend rules, if necessary!' exclaimed Nachiket.

Dharmaraj asked, 'What do you have in mind?'

'The thought of buying a fake college degree to ease getting employed has crossed my mind,' Nachiket answered.

'I can tell you today, Nachiket, if you put your mind to it, you would get a genuine degree with effort. You have a unique mind. Instead of spending on a fake a degree, invest in some tutoring. I am confident you will achieve what you want to.' the doctor said.

'It seems to me that a lot of useless information is driven into us in the name of education at colleges. They don't teach the important things, such as developing emotional maturity, or the ability to read people, or other skills that help in social interaction. They are only playing with semantics.' Nachiket felt that academics had not prepared him to meet the practical.

'You, as a discerning human being, know the difference between nonsense and sense, from your perspective. You must grant there could be others who see your idea of sense as nonsensical too. Education seems to be an exercise in semantics until it is applied. Any knowledge we cannot apply is trivia. In fact, a CEO when asked what he would pay a top-notch quizzer replied, "About the cost of a decent encyclopaedia." Applying any knowledge we gain makes us see the sense in it. But to be able to apply, you first have to make the effort of learning.'

'Yes, that could be true,' conceded Nachiket.

'If you see that as a possibility, there is scope to see any knowledge as reasonable from certain perspectives,' the doctor said, increasingly convinced that Nachiket's fears and reactions were becoming more real. 'You may disagree with, but not deny, other forms of understanding.'

'The problem, really, is when others' understanding and achievements clash with mine. They could do things to undermine me,' said Nachiket, a little diffidently. 'They may mock me about being slow…'

'You have to choose your convictions now after due diligence. Be strong and disagree when you have to… Being reasonable does not mean turning the other cheek all the time. If you anchor in a firm belief of betterment, no one would affect you at the core. If you feel taunted, step back from the situation and rehearse progressive and confident thoughts, so that the next similar situation will not affect you as much. When you are not reacting with misdirected emotions, you can apply your knowledge and experience, correctly and proactively,' advised the doctor.

'The truth is I have had this experience and it has made me lose time,' said Nachiket, still hesitant. 'It seems so cruel to hide so much from me and then reveal it only when I have lost time.'

'The truth, Nachiket, can be hard. However, do you realise you are one of the few who can see it as an actionable truth? What if I told you there are several with similar experiences, who remain deluded or desperate? Life has given you a chance to start anew. Denial of your birth-right to choose is worse than any delay.'

'I have lost so much time…can I live a life that is true now?' asked a genuinely concerned Nachiket. 'Will my life ever be without limitations?'

'Wisdom changes a person.' Dharmaraj said. 'We can only dream of going back to a carefree childhood.

We must take the responsibility to move ahead in time as adults, while nurturing what is left of the child within us. The time you have lost is insignificant compared with the time you can lose by being aware and still doing nothing. Appreciate the smallest of your achievements and challenge yourself to do bigger things gradually. Don't feel limited; choose your own reasonable and appealing concerns.'

'How can I start on a clean slate when so much has already happened?' pondered Nachiket, continuing to press the point.

'Assume for now that all you experienced, as well as your position in life today, were pre-determined…that all you are, is the result of choices you made without knowledge and that you are now in control of the choices you make *from this point forward*. OWN your life NOW, Nachiket! A chance to live anew is yours. Appreciate time. You can do with it as you wish.'

'I feel like the prisoner who, after many years in captivity, wanted to return to his cell when he was freed,' said Nachiket, apparently still sorry for himself.

'You have the knowledge and the wherewithal now,' the doctor said. 'Look forward, look outward…make small, but sure steps, and soon you will be making huge strides. Your willingness to do this will create a firm intent. Your intent will create your motivation, and your motivation will give you success. First, just be willing. The rest will follow.'

The doctor realised Nachiket could take a little more time to come to terms with his condition. Medication was controlling the positive symptoms of schizophrenia. He was having no disturbing hallucinations and his delusion had receded. However, for Nachiket to return to the mainstream, he would also need to overcome the negative symptoms of schizophrenia (such as social withdrawal, lack of motivation and the like). Dr Dharmaraj knew that with growing insight, there was danger of depression as well. Pressing questions such as *Why me?* or anxiety about the huge challenge that was just beginning could cause feelings of diffidence. The doctor decided to wait for a sure sign before resorting to the general counselling he had in mind for Nachiket. His patient first had to move from denial to acceptance, and become capable of proactively bettering his situation.

## RIGHTS AND REASONS

Let us explicitly dispense with the questions that Nachiket had, many of which are commonly found in people trying to come out of an affliction: Why? Why get started? Why should I seek betterment? Why do I need to put in any effort at all when I feel fate has dealt me a bad set of cards? Why be responsible? Why be reasonable at all, when I do not see reasonableness in my life? While we know what a reasonable outlook is, we could be hesitant or sceptical. One could ask, I think I know what I should do, but what about the way things are? Given that life seems to pit us against capable people, and face novel challenges, some of us may have doubts on whether being reasonable in this fast-paced *competitive* age is even feasible. Perhaps our 'competition' has been aware for a much longer time, making them more prepared. One could debunk life, tuck in, and ask why; wanting the whole *game* started over, with the scoreboard reset. Alternatively, we could think of short-cuts, as Nachiket did.

Life is not fair in the conventional sense. Coming to terms with reality might be more important than finding answers for every injustice. If you want to demolish the hidden harmful sheath of the mind; if you want to be constructive and enable personal purpose, if you want to experience the fulfilment that should come with it, the following sections provide clues. Reacting reasonably to our circumstances is a prerequisite to the discovery of personal purpose. Why be reasonable, righteous and resolute, despite a perceived host of reasons not to be so? There just *could be* reasons to be reasonable that are very practical. If we feel short-changed by life, as an afflicted or normal person, it could be time to try a new outlook, not merely ask 'Why?'

✳ ✳ ✳

The reason for the Grand Design of the universe, with or without other literate or intelligent life, is unknown. Whether there is a rudimentary life-form anywhere else, or any god-like caretaker(s) for this Grand Design, is also unproven. We could choose to thank or pray to, apologise to, curse and swear at... even ignore Him, Her, It or Them (whatever is responsible for us being alive). Creation IS, regardless of whether its cause is divine or mundane, because we *are* here now. A primary question, 'Who is the reason?' might only have answers in theology. The secondary query, 'Why should I be reasonable?' draws licence from the lack of a clear answer to the primary question. This query is at the core of a fundamentally misplaced rebellious spirit. Such a spirit feels there is no cause to be reasonable if no one or nothing is in charge. If no one is responsible for the creation we know, the rebel in us may conclude: what I think, say or do, cannot matter.

We need to 'unask' the question, 'Who or what is the reason?' This leads to an acceptance of our being here now, instead of a frustrating search to become something else, fashioned synthetically by social and religious standards. When the utility of living a reasonable life becomes evident, we would be able to 'unask' the question. Nachiket discusses religion later in the book. Here, I try a logical approach to support our living reasonably, instead of doing it just because of religious or social compulsions. This chapter is an attempt to persuade that being reasonable works as a survival strategy; that we need not be reasonable merely because theology, or religion, or social diktats demand that we be so. I also argue that there are reasons to be personally reasonable, despite surroundings that seem flawed.

✳ ✳ ✳

Most of us have the capability to recognise what is responsible and what is not. The most unreasonable person on the face of the Earth, if sane, is capable of recognising reasonable behaviour. Now note: irresponsibility occurs only if there are transgressions or disrespect of some generic rights or duties. Since, as intelligent humans, we can recognise responsible and irresponsible behaviour, it follows that *there probably are rights* common to all individuals.

> The most unreasonable person on the face of the Earth, if sane, is capable of recognising reasonable behaviour.

As examples of our rights, straight off the top-of-the-head, they may quite simply be:

- The right to valid information.
- The right to agree or disagree to proposed exchanges and transactions.
- The right to fair benefit in exchange of material, emotional and intellectual value.

To elaborate on these examples, when a person uses the tools of propaganda to disseminate wrong information, he or she transgresses the first right. When a person forces the exchange of goods and services, without the knowledge and agreement of another, the person transgresses the second right. Finally, when we cannot benefit mentally or materially from the value we have to offer, the third right is transgressed.

We can best understand the responsibility to be reasonable by appreciating such inherent rights that we all possess. Consider that those who are unreasonable, despite their wrongdoings, would also desire such rights in their favour. Everyone is likely to want these, regardless of their faith, or social stature, or on whichever side of the moral divide they feel they belong. Hence, they are probably universal.

Let us hazard that rights like the ones proposed define civilised behaviour, and can be offered in defence of being personally reasonable. The power to distinguish between reasonable and unreasonable behaviour is already in us. Whether a person chooses to act unreasonably (transgressing the rights of others) or reasonably (respecting the rights of others), depends on the pull of a personally realised greater good over any destructive bias.

Having said that, consider there are several convincing reasons and pressures to be unreasonable and transgress these rights. For instance, ironically, a belief in a benevolent and forgiving universe or force, may lead to perverseness as such a force cannot possibly hold people accountable. It is a logical somersault from the argument that if the universal creative force were malevolent or maleficent, then, what we do may be inconsequential. Constant change is another reason for being unreasonable. When the rules change constantly, people see no reason to be reasonable. Today, I have a job; tomorrow the company might lay me off due to downsizing or fraud. The Hollywood comedy, *Fun with Dick and Jane* parodied this. The couple in the movie take to robbery to maintain their lifestyle, after the CEO embezzles the company that was providing their livelihood.

Further arguments used to support being unreasonable is from beliefs that the imbalances in our world cannot be reasonably resolved. There will be rich countries and poor countries just as there are richer and poorer people. Many people find reasons to be unreasonable because of such social conditions. They perceive an injustice in the world and hence rationalise their being unreasonable. This class cannot anchor in a personally purposeful and non-relative self, as usually, they are convinced that consistent reasonableness is unnatural. Many miss out on the benefit of looking at themselves and their fortunes reasonably, supportively and compassionately.

Despite an environment that appears to be unjust and unfairly competitive from some perspectives, one *can* carve a personal niche. We can discover our niche when we let go of relative, comparative and transient reasons for us to be motivated. We get to see life as a continuous voyage of personal exploration and betterment, in some manner or another. In the next few sections, I will attempt to challenge reasons to be unreasonable from new directions. I argue there is a stronger case to be personally reasonable than unreasonable.

> We can discover our niche when we let go of relative, comparative and transient reasons for us to be motivated.

## *Section Highlights:*

- We can never get started on the path of reasonable personal purpose unless we 'unask' the question: What causes us to exist?
- Being unreasonable could seem the right way to act for some as they see the forces behind creation to be malevolent and life as a free-for-all with no rules.

- There are some common, inherent and reasonable rules or rights that everyone desires, allowing the conclusion that being reasonable is an available choice for us.
- Since such rights are desired by all people whether reasonable or unreasonable, we can use them as touchstones to test the validity of our actions.
- With the right information, being reasonable can become a state of mind and a powerful survival strategy for us.

## THE SYNTHETIC SUSPICION

Let's explore some reasons why a number of the afflicted and even supposedly normal people act unreasonably. Firstly, a person may choose to be unreasonable because he feels the whole edifice of human knowledge and understanding is an elaborate lie. Some may feel that the available information does not explain reality and hence the entire theoretical edifice is false. One could also feel that knowledge is an ever-shifting collection, with no permanence, and find this an acceptable excuse to be unreasonable. For example, a popularly held belief was that the earth was flat which has since been disproved. One could argue that since there cannot be absolute, unchanging knowledge, why bother with being reasonable. Does the human repository of information cheat us? Is the environment subjecting people to a huge knowledge hoax? But really, if all knowledge were a hoax, what you are reading now would not make sense. If all recorded human knowledge were an elaborate lie, any learning we come across will be indiscernible.

How is knowledge credible? The formation of objective meaning, in its representation by language (words or symbols), is something we take for granted. Since you can read this, and accept or reject it, literacy has meaning for you. People do choose what truth is and what a lie is in the spoken and written word. We reflect on fact and fiction, so that we can choose to make some ideas our own and disregard the rest. A majority among us do possess the faculty to distinguish between the reasonable and unreasonable. We must appreciate our capacity to select and choose information to internalise. Hence, can we discard all understanding as an unreasonable lie? A resounding: 'NO!'

Conclusion #1: Life has in it, at the very least, the scope for deriving reason and reasonableness.

To the literate, language, including the written word is not voodoo, but a *fait accompli*. It is an awesome miracle we take for granted. We already know Nature has an illiterate side, as explored in Part 1. This is the second reason that may cause some to doubt recorded reason and knowledge. Nachiket's feeling that recorded knowledge is synthetic was because language does *not* seem either instinctive or natural. *Language, especially in its written form, is unnatural.* If one is finding it hard to trust theoretical communication, it could be because of nature's illiteracy.

Conclusion #2: The reasonable side of recorded human knowledge may seem abnormal and cause unreasonableness, because our natural roots are illiterate.

Strangely, truth can also be a cause for a person to be unreasonable. This is our third reason why being unreasonable may seem appropriate to some. Scarlett

O'Hara, in the classic *Gone with the Wind*, has her decisive moment when she is hungry and impoverished. She swears, 'God as my witness, I will get through this if I have to lie and cheat… [And when I get over this] I will never go hungry again.' A bitter truth may force a person to be unreasonable. Actually, any compromise stemming from the methods of truth could be more inappropriate than a compassionate lie. The methods of truth conjure what appears to be the truth. These methods commonly determine what is eventually accepted and what is rejected, regardless of fact. A couple of examples, both a trifle contrived, could make this clearer.

A man declares a hunger-strike for a political cause. He fasts until he is at death's door. He then tries to communicate in an extremely weak state. His garbled statement seems decipherable as a desire to end the fast. His over-zealous followers deny him any compromise and delay medical support. He dies fasting. His followers tell the media he died in his hunger-strike for the cause. This is a truth. They also tell the press medical support was attempted. This is also a truth. This then is the harm in the methods of truth.

Truth, for most of us is typically deduced, rather than evident. People could therefore manipulate the methods of truth. In this case, a method of truth concealed a weak fasting man's need. It could well be that the man realised the enormous repercussions in carrying out his proposed martyrdom and actually wanted to suggest something constructive. What would have resulted instead are probably riots, infighting and social unrest. A conjured truth might become established and lead to chaos. It is not false, but it could be a manipulated and 'wrong' truth (a deceptive truth).

Now consider a man with very weak eyesight, again at death's door. He asks to see his daughter and the relatives summon her. By the time she arrives, he is gone. He, however, dies believing he has seen his daughter, because a niece impersonated her when all hope that the she would make it on time was lost. He dies smiling and peaceful, thinking it was his daughter he saw in his last few moments.

Truths arising from deductions alone, or those with no verifiable substance behind them, could cause more harm than help as in the example of the fasting man. Further, we can resolve or mitigate bitter or ugly truths best by a progressive nudge, as in the case of the dying man with weak eyesight. We possess the faculty to make a choice between an unreasonable truth and a reasonable lie. A lie that helps and is considerate would usually be harmless. Along the same lines, the truth sometimes hurts, and it would be more compassionate to lie. We refrain from commenting damagingly on a person's looks or affliction. Compassion and sensitivity are called for.

I hazard that for us to shun being unreasonable, we need to shift our reliance from what is apparently the truth to what is constructive or compassionate. We should not depend purely on the axioms we respect as truth, and shift our beliefs to axioms that reflect and promote progressive happenings

We should not depend purely on the axioms we respect as truth, and shift our beliefs to axioms that reflect and promote progressive happenings instead.

instead. This kind of outlook towards truth could mean the difference between our adopting an unreasonable or reasonable attitude.

Conclusion #3: We need to invalidate the unreasonableness or the ugly, and sometimes manipulated, truths we experience, in favour of progressive happenings… sometimes with harmless lies.

✳ ✳ ✳

As an argument favouring reasonableness, can we be anything other than reasonable towards our own selves? Then reasonableness must be natural, right? This was the good doctor's attempt to persuade Nachiket that anybody can try being reasonable. Unexplainable fate, or maybe the acts of unreasonable people, may have brought you to where you are. However, when you take that as a given, as something you have to accept, you can act and no longer just react. Suddenly, in everything there is utility instead of futility. Any vexations to the spirit become manageable. You begin to feel that the very question *Why life?* is unnatural and a synthetic suspicion. You experience living as unique—your birth, your life, and your journey forward. Now, let us consider next the categorical disclaimer: I did not choose to be born and to be a human being. Does this give us the right to be unreasonable? This is the ultimate reluctance to own life. It deserves an entire section.

*Section Highlights:*
- As an elementary argument for reasonableness, we humans do have the ability to recognise (un) reasonable behaviour.

- Some feel that reasonableness is idealistic, unnatural and synthetic because much of our reasoning is in language, and language is absent in raw Nature.
- Several ugly truths in creation could also force some to consider being unreasonable.
- We should see discouraging or unreasonable truths as inferior to progressive and constructive happenings.
- Adopting reasonableness is a key that can unlock a powerful personal purpose. It can open the way for living with a sense of success, without comparisons or doubt.

## AN ATOMIC ASSOCIATION

In a strange case, an infertile couple asked a woman to be a surrogate mother to a baby from the sperm of a donor, selected by them. This led to a legal tangle after the couple broke up. Courts had to conform to laws and precedents, and could not determine who was responsible for the nurture of the child. They could not pin it on the infertile 'father' or 'mother,' the surrogate mother, or the anonymous donor[38]. Society brought an orphan into existence because a couple used the capabilities of modern medical science to 'conceive,' while the courts had to respect individual rights and legal precedents. How do we explain such a birth? Perhaps it is just one of those puzzles for humankind to ponder on. Seeing puzzles of this kind may cause

---

[38] Reported on 2 February 1998 in *The Hindu* a national Indian newspaper, based on a US news agency report.

an afflicted individual to question the reason for his existence, or to pass the buck and the blame.

If we feel our predecessors made the decision for us to exist, look at the natural choice we all made. All of us emerged from the union of an egg and a very determined sperm, beating odds of millions-to-one. Looking at a possible exception in science to this concept only makes the choice more profound. This exception is a procedure called Intra Cytoplasmic Sperm Injection (ICSI). A group of maverick doctors first performed ICSI in 1992. The doctors inject sperm into an egg using a special pipette. The pipette sucks in the head of the sperm containing the genetic coding after cutting off its tail. This pipette is then pierced into the egg and the sperm released. ICSI claims successful impregnation in cases with very low sperm counts and virtually no motility (ability of sperm to swim).

We can argue that a sperm cell in such a procedure exercises no choice. However, consider that there is a drive to exist regardless of the method of fertilisation. Even if we were all test-tube babies, we would still exhibit an inborn choice to live. The embryo's innate tendency to develop is an expression of an instinctive choice to come alive. Once activated, the *need* of the package of genetic information to develop into a baby seems inherent. In other words, no fertilised egg self-destructs. Whatever the odds, there is a drive to exist regardless of the being's chances to perform well in its environment. An example is the Rhesus factor conflict where a fertilised egg still 'wants' to exist despite the intolerance of the birthing environment[39]. We might be able to consider therefore that a deeper choice to live is nascent in the sperm and egg. This package seems to exercise a choice to be born.

At first reckoning, the choice of an embryonic cell to develop seems no different from lower life-forms, or some mindless force. The distinction is in recognising that this single cell has in it the blueprint of a thinking feeling and complex life-form, with the potential to contemplate the mysteries of the universe. In regression to its beginnings, our mind existed in a nascent form. Perhaps it knew no words or meaning, but it had enough individual drive to play out its creation. It chose to exist when it had the chance to do so.

This throws up the questions: Why should a person with a challenging disability be born? Why would parents choose to bring a child with a congenital disability into the world when it could invite cruelty? This is where we must acknowledge the mission over the mistake. We have to view the blemishes and conflicts in living as puzzles or missions for humankind. Just as the example of the orphan child we began this section with, such births could be problems for us to resolve in the long run. They are questions posed by time for human development to answer. They are missions, which beg humanity to realise that despite different points of view, we must yet cooperate as a

> We have to view the blemishes and conflicts in our lives as missions for humankind.

---

[39] The Rh-disease occurs when there is an incompatibility between the blood types of the mother and the foetus.

race. We, although with some debate it inevitably invites, can realise these are not *divine* mistakes (See the text box: "Design, Default or Deviation").

In the forthcoming chapters, The Hidden Navigator, and Clarity in Control, I share some ideas that have helped me find a balance amongst what to depend on and what to be concerned about, and also consider what one can influence personally in humankind's mission. Denying any stake at all in our own creation, flaws and all, is the denial of our power to do, learn, and enjoy in life. It might be as important to accept the *experience* of mistakes as it is to experience triumphs, individually and as a race.

Conclusion #4: Being born has an element of choice, however minuscule, and our accepting this possibility could make the difference between regretful unreasonableness and mature responsibility in our outlook.

The four conclusions outlined are meant to reassure that we can be reasonable and succeed; that we need not see our situation, whether normal or afflicted, as one that demands devious effort. I emphasize, this is a prerequisite for donning life's obligations or missions reasonably; that we need to own life, flaws and all, for us to progress. We need never compare ourselves and our situation with anyone, whatever are the pluses and minuses of our reality package. You are a distinct being who has never existed before and never will exist again. You are an association of atoms unlike any that was or will ever be. You are an absolute fact in the scheme of Creation. No person, no twin, no clone, is exactly like you. You could get volumes of comparisons on your looks, attitudes, and skills, with things real and fictional. Still, nothing compares to you and your life. Dharmaraj sought to highlight this point for Nachiket.

> Realise your absolute, non-relative and unique standing.

This is the second key outlook of the book for us: Realise your absolute, non-relative and unique standing. Emblazon this too in your mind.

---

### *Design, Default or Deviation*

*A related and controversial issue is the continuing debate on abortion between pro-life and pro-choice groups. There could be many reasons for opting to terminate a mistake of 'cohabiting.' Amongst these is the reason that the life-form cannot be cared for in the circumstances. Could this primal being have been born to live a full life without harming itself or its circle of humanity? Can humanity be the judge of that? The Bible says, 'Thou shalt not kill;' it, prima facie, begs the argument, 'Thou shalt allow to be born;' or, does it?*

*John Donohue (Stanford Law School) & Steven Levitt (The University of Chicago) reached some novel conclusions in their paper 'The Impact of Legalized Abortion on Crime', in* The Quarterly Journal of Economics *dated May 2001. They attributed as much as half the sharp drop in American crime rates in the 1990's, to the 1973 Roe vs. Wade decision by the Supreme Court, legalising abortion throughout the USA. When linked to peak criminal activity in the age 18-24, the sequential drop in crime rates in each of the States follows their sequential adoption of legalised abortion. The research suggests that abortion of a*

> *foetus with lesser chances for social success could pre-empt criminal activity later in life.*
>
> *There is inexcusable ignorance or deliberate stupidity at the root of this debate. Modern science provides us with enough options, to prevent such dilemmas. If we reject rigid beliefs or religious orthodoxy, and favour social stability for the agents, their progeny and our community instead, we will see a 'greater good' in taking prophylactic steps. Given the fact of our empowerment by law, we seem to have the right to take either decision. Any decision within a time frame pre-empting discernible human features, such as the sex of the embryo, does seem faultless. If we can take the responsibility to create a primal being, we may be able to take the responsibility for terminating it before it becomes manifest, despite the fact of its primal drive to exist. Still, there are no conclusive arguments favouring one side over the other. We have to choose and abide by whatever we choose, without fear of human or divine retribution as the basis for our choices.*

## <u>*Section Highlights:*</u>

- People who question life instead of accepting and acting in it are generally unreasonable and destructive.
- There is an element of personal choice in our being born, even when it is rationalised and reduced to a miniscule one.
- Accepting this element could mean the difference between owning and enjoying life or being reckless and irresponsible in it.

- Successful living also depends on owning one's life, and having faith in life's abundance for the unique you, in some manner or another.
- We must realise that each one of us is so unique that nothing and no one was, is or will ever be just like us.

## JUDO JUDGMENTS

We have a body of research that suggests a sound rationale for us to be reasonable in our dealings, despite any affliction or sense of inadequacy. Though

> There is no enduring justification, theoretical or practical, for world-views that promote corrupt or unreasonable action.

some aspects in our existential deck seem stacked against being *good* and reasonable, the success of unreasonableness appears short-lived. There is no enduring justification, theoretical or practical, for world-views that promote corrupt or unreasonable action. Therefore, being reasonable is not merely for us to conform to social or religious correctness. Instead, it is because the success of other survival strategies seems susceptible to friction, psychosocial conflict and other breakdowns of personal and social security. An unrelenting aggressive stance in our dealings may lead to internecine conflict and eventually, a collective self-destruction.

Consider this information sourced from the book, *The One Percent Advantage* on the findings of John Maynard Smith (1920–2004), a pre-eminent academician[40]. He was responsible for pioneering work on *evolutionarily stable strategy*. He mathematically proved that in societies, where aggressive encounters are more than a rarity, the average outcome is decline. A mixed society, however, comprising both aggressive *and passive* individuals, would result in stability. The growth and proportion of aggressive and passive individuals in a mixed society tends to remain stable. This is probably because the passive individuals survive encounters through defensive strategies. The aggressive individuals, in contrast, injure their own kind due to infighting. The researchers used communities of hawks and doves in their studies.

In addition to inferences from the preceding work, we can also draw some allied conclusions from the work of Robert Axelrod and William D Hamilton (1935–2000). They developed survival strategies that faced off in a computer game (similar to chess programmes). They built different behavioural models, including strategies such as doing exactly the opposite of what your opponent does, and players acting randomly. Running several variations of the game turned up a strategy that led to victory. They called it Tit-for-Tat. It had only two rules: On the first move, cooperate; afterwards, respond by doing exactly what your opponent did. Tit-for-Tat, according to Robert Trivers, on whose work the modelling was based, is 'a strategy

---

[40]    Gribben, John and Mary. *The One Percent Advantage*. Boston: Twayne Publishers, 1988

of cooperation based on reciprocity.' Dr Trivers is one of the most influential evolutionary theorists of this age[41].

There was a second round of computer simulation, involving sixty-two entries designed to meet the challenge of beating the Tit-for-Tat strategy. The simulation iterated over three million choices. This came up with the same result. Tit-for-Tat was further refined to *forgive* one more unfriendly act. It ignored an opponent's unfriendly act for a second time, offering cooperation once more before resorting to copying the other player's approach. This refinement made the strategy work still more successfully. It is an 'evolutionarily stable strategy' with a vengeance. The strategy works as an effective tool in interactions. It is also a reasonable choice. Like Judo, it uses the opponent's own moves against him.

Purposeful living would be a series of reasonable choices that develop progressive *karma*. Responding in the same measure, though the response may seem uncivil, is the only proviso that could be an acceptable compromise of the reasonable. Responding in the same manner is personally purposeful, and a progressive survival strategy. Dharmaraj made it clear in his dialogues that he was not asking Nachiket to turn the other cheek all the time. We will see how to apply 'cooperative reciprocity' practically a little later.

---

[41] Dr Robert Trivers is a Professor of Anthropology and Biological Sciences at Rutgers University, USA. Trivers proposed the theory of reciprocal altruism in 1971.

The two ideas posited in the preceding sections are that there should be a willingness to own life, and, that this leads to a reasonable outlook. These sections tried a logical approach to set the grounds for reasonableness as a survival strategy. Real reasonableness requires a shift in perspective, a realisation that you can accept your circumstances and change them if required…that you get to the point where you can declare you are not a victim, whether afflicted or normal.

If we understand that we must accept and act on life's conflicts—personal, professional and social—we have discovered the secret to being motivated. But then, being reasonable and motivated at all times is hard in the face of some of life's challenges. Some of these challenges may seem unreasonable and unjust. What if changing our situation seems impossible, even when we are willing to try? What is our takeaway when our circumstances take an interminably long time to change, if they do change at all? How can we attempt being reasonable when our challenges seem impossible to get over? A brief discussion on 'Challenge' is in our next chapter.

## *Section Highlights:*

- Popular standards tend to promote aggression and confrontation as traits that display confidence.
- Many downplay the role of peaceable reasonableness as a successful survival strategy.
- Some scientific research, however, seem to indicate that reasonableness and selective cooperation are the best survival strategies.

- The only unfairness that seems 'acceptable' is when we respond in the same vein, after offering cooperation a couple of times—a strategy called *cooperative reciprocity*.

**9**

# CHALLENGE

'**I** have to keep this meeting short,' said Dr Dharmaraj. 'I understand you wanted to meet me urgently…' The doctor was beginning to worry that Nachiket was growing dependent on him, and wanted to wean him away as he was showing improvement.

'I have just a few quick questions,' responded Nachiket. 'I am still not sure why I have the challenge of this condition. Challenge is ubiquitous—in youth, and in old age.'

'Even more reason to see that it has a purpose,' explained the doctor. 'Every challenge, big and small, has a lesson hidden inside it; a special learning that you acquire when you do not buckle under it.'

'Why should life be so? Going from challenge to challenge? Isn't there an easier way to teach?' inquired Nachiket.

'What if I told you that there was some knowledge meant for you that no one else would get? The learning is very exclusive and personal. Life gives lessons to each according to one's own need.'

'Is there a point where challenges end?' asked Nachiket.

'When challenges end, the guiding force in us no longer exists.' Dharmaraj said with finality. 'Challenge provides us with choices of directions to take and destinations to seek. When we move towards these destinations, the benefits become obvious.'

'My purpose seems to be in the challenge I choose…' said Nachiket, beginning to understand.

'… Or in the challenges bestowed on you,' completed the doctor. 'For example, consider that your condition has provided you with a unique opportunity to view life from a new perspective.'

'I know some things several others don't….' said a clued-up Nachiket.

'Exactly!' the doctor said.

'I suddenly feel lonely, and the prospect of an entire life looming ahead of me… fighting challenges… growing old…' switched Nachiket, a little despondently.

'Every day is an opportunity to learn.' The doctor responded. 'You have had this experience. Already you are learning from it, and I have no doubt you will do well. You see obstacles where I see opportunities.'

'But we do get older…' said Nachiket, thinking of the challenges of old age. 'What is the opportunity when instead of getting better, we get worse?'

'Change the perspective,' the doctor replied. 'The fact is, although we seem worse off in some respects as we get older, we do get better in others. You must focus on the things you can do and the learning you inevitably acquire, and, which I anticipate you will share.'

'Does this mean my betterment will extend into old age?' Nachiket asked.

The doctor clarified. 'The yardsticks by which you measure betterment need to change. Today you may focus on physical and material goals. Later on in life, emotional and spiritual goals may become as important. It is only a change in perspective to the basic direction of getting better continuously. Think about it.'

The doctor did not tinker with his prescription. Nachiket only had real doubts about existence. This was a clear sign that he was out of his delusional world. It was likely he would settle into a normal life. His concerns about getting old were no different from those of a normal person. The doctor allayed Nachiket's fears with explanations and suggested some reading[42]. Dharmaraj advised the parents to keep up the medication and take Nachiket out to informal social gatherings, or places where he would not feel threatened.

## THE HIDDEN NAVIGATOR

Is life an accident in the cosmos? Is intelligence a deviation from the norms of Nature? Should people just stop questioning and exist, as Sartre, seems to have suggested? Does living have a point? Does it need to have a point? Several of us have considered these questions sometime in our lives. A great many of us

---

[42]  See GLP4 "Find Gold in Old" at the end of the book under Good Living Practices

also dismiss such questions and get on with our affairs, preparing breakfast, passing the sauce, and paying the bills. While the questions seem passé given the exhilarating pace of this age, they acquire significance because this quicker pace brings novel challenges. When an afflicted individual confronts such challenges, he usually questions why they are there.

Adverse changes in our circumstances could create perceptions of unreasonable challenge. In some challenging settings, a person may feel ill-equipped. Yet other circumstances test a person's comfort zone severely. While this can occur for any individual, it is common for a person with schizophrenia. Due to his bizarre experiences, Nachiket apparently saw never-ending challenges instead of opportunities. He was treading water instead of swimming. Like several out there, he was asking, 'Why this kind of challenge? Why do I lack clear abilities when others seem to be well-equipped? Why do others find it necessary to challenge me? Why do challenges keep disturbing the comfort I have with myself? Why is life challenging?' Let's see how we can view challenge positively.

As an explanation for challenge, I first go on the beaten track. The 'bad' and challenging elements of life may arguably be some kind of deliberate design flaw. Just as the bigger trials and tribulations are missions for humankind, the more bite-sized ones may be for us to resolve as individuals. Perhaps this is the Creator's, or Nature's, way of getting us ready for the long haul. Readiness is having the mental state to face our unique reality. For example, a surgeon should practise to be ready and not get sick at the sight of blood. Small challenges like this could be like the prick and intent of a vaccine, which develops our ability to meet bigger, similar challenges. In the readiness to accept small challenges is the preparation to take on bigger problems. The key is to recognise that we are consistently better equipped to face bigger challenges as we face smaller ones, and to treat *that* as *manna*. By running from problems and challenges, we reject the gifts they bring with them, which usually are subtle and intangible.

*** * ***

The Japanese, in the past, used to have the concept of lifetime employment. How did it work? How do you get people to work productively without threatening them with losing their income or livelihood? When asked how they handled the shirkers, one manager replied, 'We gave them a chair, a desk, and possibly a window. Not a single shred of work went their way. They were not socially isolated, but made to feel that time hangs heavy. In most cases, they either started looking for things to do after a while, or left to do something on their own.' People can degenerate and decay, or improve and flourish from a null state, as suggested in the foregoing example.

Challenge is the appearance of a middle ground that provides a *recognisable choice of direction* in life. The problems we grasp as

Challenge is the appearance of a middle ground that provides a *recognisable choice of direction* in life.

our own and seek to solve, provide us with a sense of purpose. Take away the 'bad' and the challenging, and people would be direction-less. We could go the distance without going anywhere. No beginning, no end, and nothing in between. What would exist is a uniform aimlessness, or perhaps a competent, but dormant state. Introduce challenges, and *presto*—we have direction.

Now consider that an awkward past has caused a difficult challenge in the present. In addition to the challenges from demanding elements in the present, some may feel they cannot run from their past. They may think they are committed and can do nothing as they are a product of their past. To change the past is impossible and in the realm of fantasy. Nevertheless, raising our fists heavenwards to demand explanations for our troubled past may not be the answer. We can take comfort instead by believing that whatever happened would not have happened if it were not feasible in the order of things.

That we can be challenged, acquire learning, and have direction from a 'bad' experience is seldom accepted or understood. It sounds better to say, 'We must tackle problems, learn from our experience, and strive to improve,' which is the same thing. Pause a moment to recall the three most dreadful things that have happened in your life. Once you have done this, think next of the three most wonderful things. Now read the footnote[43]. Whatever the challenge, there is always something to be learned. Such learning is sometimes latent and actualises later. Everything is experience

---

[43]  Which came easier? The negative is generally more likely. We do remember our lessons.

waiting for alignment. Nobody can explain how this happens. We know when we keep ourselves open and ready. We need to be patient as we persevere.

✳ ✳ ✳

Life is like the lifetime employment of old-world Japan. Either people find something to do, or they slowly but surely, opt out of the wheel of life. It is easy to consider this and to say 'How true,' sitting back on a comfortable chair, sipping a cup of tea, with electricity powering your house. However, it is *very hard to accept a purpose that seems to be someone else's*. We can find a great deal of things requiring attention, but we simply fail to personalise such requirements due to perceived limitations. Many claim, 'That's not my job' instead, because their ego cannot accept a purpose they have not created. Everything is a chore when one has not discovered or accepted one's purpose. If we feel we lack direction, the remedy lies in choosing challenges of interest, and adopting these challenges as part of our purpose. Challenge is a navigator when viewed with the right perspective.

Life is not about letting it slip by, but doing what we can, when we can do it. You may get results now, a year from now, or ten years from now. When we recognise and *accept* our purpose in the present, we will attract the things that overcome the past and help fulfil this purpose. This is not magical. You just are more likely to notice the things that can help you progress when you are focused with a purpose. You get into the flow more readily. First, accept the facts. Second, influence what you can to make it better.

> ### *CRUEL CHALLENGES*
>
> *As we saw in the previous chapter, in the section* An Atomic Association, *some challenges, like Alzheimer's, seem to border on inexplicable cruelty. Can anybody ever develop the empathy necessary to get inside the heads of those who face such challenges? We find stories of remarkable courage among those who choose to share their experience. Yet, their core is perhaps impenetrable. Hidden in their pain, affliction or condition, there just could be awareness and sensitivity far beyond anything any ordinary person can realise.*
>
> *Some might feel that their being singled out or the isolation they experience is unfair, but all of us, the ordinary and the challenged, live in separate personal worlds. There is no total understanding of any one by another. Still, we can reach out. We are often surprised when we do reach out eventually. Challenges such as unfortunate experiences, disease and disability could exist to encourage us as a race to reach out to one another.*

Enlarging our concerns and donning a bigger role in the things that concern us makes personal purpose evident. In this role, we learn to distinguish a life well rewarded from a rewarding life. Once we discover such a distinction, we can anchor in it firmly. Be grateful for the progress you make, and the rewarding insights you accrue, as you accept challenge and define your purpose.

Life is not the world of Sartre, or the world of a mad scientist with your brain hooked into some 'reality machine'. The world is yours. If you can think, use it. If you can move, use it. If you can see, use it. If you can talk, use it. You will walk the path of our species and society as you do your unique and personal walk of life. You are living for yourself and your concerns. *Carpé Diem*. Seize the day. If we recognise the progress we make, and do not subscribe to comparative rewards, our sense of wellness endures. The third mantra, and yet another 'gutsy' key principle from the book to adopt is, 'Know [your] betterment in every circumstance.' Emblazon this also in gold on your mind.

This is all okay for a younger person, some would say. The feeling of gradual betterment is almost self-evident if you are young enough. Nachiket was projecting into the future when he asked how people could be proactive when they are older. Their strength and mental abilities seem to be getting worse instead of better. We can offset growing older to an extent. It is never too late to learn new skills. Find that quality which brings your years of living into sharp focus. This is the difference between having fifty years of experience, and seeing oneself as having five years of experience, ten times around. In several ways, we can refuse to degenerate and decay by finding new yardsticks for personal success. We explore this in the next GLP 'Find Gold in Old.' There is scope for hope in every moment of life.

## *Section Highlights:*

- Being reasonable could be difficult when faced with challenges that appear insurmountable.

- However, without challenges, big or small, there is only uniform aimlessness, or a state in which our competencies remain dormant.
- When we lack direction, we must adopt challenges for us to tackle and improve.
- When we adopt and respect challenge as a part of our existential purpose, there is learning and direction.
- Challenge can be a navigator when viewed with the right perspective.
- As we get older, challenges change. We should adapt and choose new ones.

# 10

# TRADITION

'The problem seems not so much with my delusion now, but with some actions in the past that I now regret. For instance, I feel guilty about transgressing some religious beliefs. Perhaps what I experienced is a retribution for this.' Nachiket said which further indicated to the doctor that he was well on the path to normality.

Dharmaraj responded, 'Religion is always personal. Personal choice should dictate the extent of your religious beliefs and practise of these beliefs. In our humdrum world, it may not always be feasible to stick to all of the religious practices. Still, we need not feel guilty.'

'Religion dictates so much ritual and protocol. I think they must have a purpose. These tenets could not have been handed down blindly from generation to generation,' said Nachiket.

'You could be right,' conceded the doctor. 'However, it is useful to keep in mind that they were handed down from long ago and are dissimilar in different faith. There is no commonality in ritual. Yet, every religion does provide existential explanations as a safety net, before we can rely on our competence. For many, if it were not for religion, all would be bleak until they discover their own hope and motivation. Religion provides purpose until purpose becomes your religion.'

'Are the several claims of an ultimate human fate, self-realisation, or heaven and hell just imaginary?' Nachiket asked, expressing a common doubt.

'Not necessarily,' said the doctor, again choosing his words carefully. 'All I am saying is living that aligns oneself, one's personal life, work, and community is all that matters. Our ultimate fate need not concern us now. What matters is to live a life of reasonable and constructive choices today without feeling anxious about an ultimate reward and punishment. Even if states like enlightenment exist, they are beyond current understanding. Instead of being apprehensive of the unknown and following religious beliefs out of fear or guilt, we can do so by choice. By the same licence, we can also choose to debunk the entire religious razzmatazz if we find it unhelpful.'

'What if I choose and then cannot follow everything?' queried Nachiket.

'There is still no need for guilt,' the doctor said emphatically. 'If you are following a reasonable, constructive and personal purpose, there can be no wrongdoing. When you begin to believe in a progressive mission, unique yet shareable, the mission enables you to make the right choices. Hence, your actions, quite spontaneously, would align with a progressive, productive and positive purpose, conservative or liberal.'

Nachiket began to get agitated. 'My guilt is beyond anything you can understand. Religion is just a part of it. You can't imagine what I have done to others around me because of my callous attitude! I used to feel I was not answerable for anything I did. Now that I am awake to a true reality, there seems to be a lot to regret.'

A tear rolled down Nachiket's cheek. The doctor felt this could be the turning point. Nachiket was ready to understand something bothering him deep down in a new light. Dharmaraj extended and placed his hand on Nachiket's. 'You can tell me about it. I am with you.'

Nachiket spoke with a catch in his throat. 'I have done plenty of things that are just plain wrong and have probably hurt numerous people. How do I come to terms with these deeds? I missed so many relationships that could have been fulfilling. You tell me this is all fated. In that case, I would be the unluckiest person alive. I seem to be unlucky in aspects of love. I lost my grandfather before I could tell him how much I loved and admired him. I lost a girl I loved when I got the disability. I feel I was thoughtless in many ways. I think I emotionally abused so many others. Now that I am recovering, I should feel better, but I feel terrible instead. How could I have been that way? Now I can never go back to correct what went wrong.'

It was a cathartic release, and the doctor spoke kindly. 'Underlying forces over which you had no control influenced you. Do not blame yourself for this. What's done is done, and belongs in the past. Love goes only when it wants to teach you to love better. I am afraid there is no technique that can make good the loss of a love. All you can do is to build good memories from this point on. You should not see the future as an extension of your past. Let me share a couple of ideas on coping with loss.'

The doctor highlighted some points to help Nachiket tackle his sense of loss[44]. Nachiket then grew composed. 'I am sorry,' he said, wiping his tears and sitting upright.

'Don't feel bad,' said the doctor reassuringly. 'Expressing valid emotions is not wrong. If I know you, you have made up your mind. You have the ability to explore emotions fully, but you also need to make sure you let go that which is not relevant for today…'

'I feel much better now. It is as if a weight has lifted,' said Nachiket.

'It is common to attribute everything bad to oneself alone,' the doctor explained. 'Instead, treat your past, good or bad, as fate. As things slip into the past, they no longer have complete power. You can now make proactive choices and face up to whatever is ahead. You must trust time to heal any limitations you still feel. They would heal, as you appreciate the unique relationship you have with the external world. Stand up and be counted among those who grasp life with confidence. You have it in you.'

'I know what I must do and I can do it. Is there anything else you have to say, or anything we have left unexplored?' Nachiket looked at the doctor squarely.

'Nothing!' exclaimed the doctor. 'Go ahead and grab your new life with enthusiasm. I know a very good counsellor who will be able to help you handle habitual discouraging thoughts. Take these meetings as the last miles in your recovery.'

---

[44]  See GLP5 "Beginning to Start Over" at the end of the book under Good Living Practices

'Can I come and see you whenever I want?' asked Nachiket.

'You only need to see me as a friend, not a doctor. Write to me.' The doctor smiled. 'We will keep in touch to ensure all remains well, and also for your prescriptions. I wish you the very best!'

Dr Dharmaraj had not been the typical psychiatrist, just prescribing medication and waiting for the cessation of symptoms. He had acknowledged that the larger world was not perfect, something which is obvious to most of us. We still carry on nonetheless. Nachiket conceivably, had felt the need to adopt his peculiar outlook in order to workaround his perception that he and his surroundings were inadequate. He had fabricated a mental sanctuary to protect himself. Dharmaraj had crossed over to Nachiket's world and looked outward with him, sitting by his side. He had not confronted him or tried to disprove his delusions logically. He had waited for Nachiket to gain insight, just nudging his thinking and removing his fears.

There was a whole, but timid person in Nachiket waiting to feel free. If he could only take ownership of his life, he would be safe and perhaps he could even be among the 40 per cent of the afflicted that get back to the mainstream. Though Nachiket seemed less confident now than before, Dr Dharmaraj reassured the parents that his inner strength was growing. He was ready to face his fears instead of hiding in an artificial cocoon of false beliefs.

The doctor insisted Nachiket should keep taking his medication. Perhaps at some time in the future, Dr Dharmaraj might consider a 'medication holiday' or resort to placebos, to test whether the functioning of the brain had stabilised. The doctor had found that in some clients, just the initial push to stability, with short-term medication was often enough. However, for now, medication was Nachiket's lifeline to reality. As to the discouraging thoughts that seemed to creep in despite his new understanding, the doctor referred Nachiket to a counsellor. What remained was to change some ways of harmful thinking that had become a habit.

## BATON OR VAULTING POLE

Why did Nachiket find it necessary to discuss tradition and then his relationships? Traditions cause confusion mainly in two areas: ritualistic acknowledgements of the existence of God, and, roles and relationships between and among genders. Sometimes there is a lot of personal unrest in these areas. Conflicts in these are often the trigger for episodes of crisis in schizophrenia patients[45]. Traditions form a major part of our historical learning. However, many traditional beliefs may seem confusing, sometimes even barbaric. In addition to twisted tradition, the sensitive schizophrenia patients sometimes imagine their relationships are being threatened by critics and rivals. Some conclude erroneously, based on outdated traditional fiats, that their relationships or beliefs are immoral. Should we then conclude that all tradition is unviable with no role in the present? Should we challenge history and our

---

[45] Crisis episodes, in the case of schizophrenia, are a sudden precipitation of symptoms including blatant displays of odd behaviour

interpretations of what is moral or immoral? How can we feel comfortable with traditional beliefs, if following them seems artificial, or in conflict with reason? How can we apply some of our personal insights, when our relationships with others seem subject to threats or feelings of guilt? Perhaps a rational explanation for creation and relationships outside traditional bounds would help.

✳ ✳ ✳

Traditional thinking affects everybody, whether we are followers or not. Some social factions declare that traditional rituals, handed down over the ages, are mandatory for balanced living. Such diktats are a part of the collective mnemonic too. Many of us adopt an unquestioning belief to the extent that we feel uneasy and fearful if we skip traditional rituals. Elders state that there are reasons for these practices, and that to question them is blasphemy. Still, for some, following traditional beliefs, ceremony and ritual, or avoiding them, could be like trying to leap backward or forward. I say that because the question as to which state is better is wide open. The best state is a stable state. For us to be stable requires intellectual or emotional commitment. Dr Dharmaraj does not say it in so many words, but this is his point. He wants Nachiket to be comfortable with his level of traditional practice.

Faith and religion are in our roots, and it is impossible to imagine a world without them. When people seek explanations, faith and religion attempt answers. The several explanations of Creation provided in tradition often act as support systems in our upbringing. Religion and faith provide a place to stand on long before the realisation of their enormous promise. If they cannot convince, some religious ideas even confuse, just to provide security. Sometimes, they seem illogical, but we still follow them as they are comforting. Most beliefs intend to safeguard, just as a child's crib is meant to protect, not imprison. Or, they can perhaps be the scaffolding, which help us in constructing a personal world-view.

The basis for Nachiket's delusion was belief in the existence of a supreme state and rebirth. The mind cannot resolve the existence of a supreme being and a personal soul without bringing in all the associated baggage of spirits, demons, and demigods. If people can conceive of a God, then why shouldn't we consider the rest? This leads us back to the magical-religious aspects of ritual—what it heralds or wards away. Ritual, with its associated symbolism, usually makes a deep impact on the psyche. For believers, it creates a helpful force within. It allows them to face the vicissitudes of life with equanimity and a sense of protection. Life spares the non-believers the entire paradigm. They just go about existing, praising or blaming only themselves and the real environment. It is for those who are not quite believers or non-believers that ambivalent feelings about ritual and tradition occur.

For the unsure, as Nachiket was after he came out of his delusion, one can propose that we view Creation as a property of existence. Just as heat is a property of fire, Creation is a property of 'is-ness,' nothing more. Also, just as heat has behind it something hot like a fire, Creation is a manifestation of an *a priori* force.

Because we experience this manifestation, we can conclude there is a force, or a force behind a force, or a force behind a force behind a force, *ad infinitum*. In other words, because we cannot wish away this manifestation, we cannot wish away the existence of a force, whatever be the levels upon levels on which it comes stacked. You could call this force Nature, or call it God. It permeates all that is matter, energy, space, and time.

A rational argument favouring the possibility of the existence of God goes thus. The non-believers can only claim there *may not* be a God, but cannot—and probably do not—claim there *is* no God. They cannot claim God did not exist in the past or will not exist in the future or that a Force does not exist elsewhere. This is because none of us have experienced all of time and space. Time is a dimension too according to scientists, which must mean that God *might* exist somewhere, sometime and at the *same* time! Absence of evidence is not evidence of absence[46]. This is a comforting thought for believers, because this argument negates the God *does not exist* hypothesis, while allowing for the rationalist's argument: God *may not exist*.

Most conflicts in theology, however, are not from such a core dichotomy of existence or non-existence of God. They usually arise out of interpretations that portray a 'God' with all the foibles of a mortal (for example, a jealous God). Religious clashes and claims by purists that one point of view is superior to another seem licenced by this view of the divine. But forcing isolating religious beliefs on another, or refusing to celebrate

---

[46]   Carl Sagan (1934–96)

other understanding, may be just one step away from fanaticism. The use of fear, force or hype to perpetrate isolating beliefs is the cause

> One person's faith seems superstition to another.

of much of our social unrest and conflicts, in both the afflicted and the normal. One person's faith seems superstition to another.

Entire societies could base their functioning on values promoting one-upmanship and victory over other forms of understanding. For example, some interpret the Quran as declaring that true Islam cannot accept other religions. There have supposedly been instances of immigration officials searching and confiscating non-Islamic religious texts and pictures at the point of entry into some Islamic countries.

How can we, as afflicted or normal individuals, feel motivated in an obviously splintered world? How can we resolve conflicts in us that may arise from differences in the practices and teachings of different beliefs? How can we feel personally aligned in our outlook, despite having made different choices?

We can subsume the apparent conflicts amongst various schools of ideological thought by a personal commitment to the greater good. We can have different beliefs, and yet be humane, caring and considerate to one another and our home in the cosmos. What we commonly do, despite diverse beliefs, is to nurture that which Is, in the way we want to. We can nurture it as a divine power or a mundane Force. If you want to praise It in a church, mosque or temple, or any other way, go ahead. If you see it in Nature and want to be a rabid ecologist, go ahead. If you feel science holds the answers, look inwards, outwards, and every way feasible at this manifestation of the Force. Any belief or ritual that does this, and does not go against humane principles, is likely to be civilised and valid.

A simple test for our personal traditional style, although we may not be practising several of its tenets, can be our comfort and personal resolve towards it. For example, consider that a Muslim is able to perform the discipline of the *Namaaz* or a Hindu is able to perform a *Vedic* ritual, or a follower of Christ is able to attend Mass or service, without feeling coerced into it. This reflects the strength of personal commitment and subscription to faith. Those practising tradition and faith should be able to do without the validation of others. If some people lack traditional beliefs, they need not be disparaging in their manner towards those who practise any constructive and progressive faith of their choosing, as also *vice-versa*.

In conclusion, when we have a different lifestyle and cannot subscribe with conviction to any faith, it can be liberating for us to realise that as long as our actions promote betterment and a greater good, there is no need for any guilt. We can achieve a personal, communal, or other meaningful goal feeling the same sense of commitment to a greater good. If a person is bettering himself, and being constructive as a believer or a non-believer, living can be guiltless. When we don this responsibility to make things better, we transcend conflict. Tradition is therefore both a baton to pass on and a vaulting pole to release after we make the jump. Treat it suitably.

<u>*Section Highlights:*</u>
- The two remaining aspects that could affect our outlook are traditional beliefs, and the physical and emotional impact they may have in our relationships.
- Traditional beliefs could be an important foundation to forming one's own unique worldview, but some cause feelings of fear or guilt.
- The extent to which we conform to traditional beliefs and practise rituals should result from personal choice. Force, fear or hype cannot be the basis.
- When we, in any way or form, nurture and celebrate Creation, we can be guiltless and feel abundant, whatever be the extent of our explicit traditional practice.
- When we don a responsibility to make our world better, as supporters of tradition or otherwise, we can transcend meaningless conflict.

## THE SEXUAL SKIRMISH

There is a delicate area in tradition, with a huge, awkward legacy within the collective mnemonic—that of gender roles and relations. These sometimes contribute to the onset of schizophrenia. In this section, I extend some cursory explanations on partnerships to try and help the afflicted and the sensitive resolve simple glitches in their relationships. The advice on relationships shared in the following paragraphs is very much in passing as compared with specialised books on the topic. The intent is to outline important aspects on the 'war of the sexes' and on maintaining relationships. It cannot replace counselling, but throws some light on some of the more obvious issues in relationships. We can refuse to be hostages of past failures in interacting and can develop the ability to be secure in our interactions going forward.

✳ ✳ ✳

Stability in roles and relationships with a significant other, if that be our choice, is important for recognising and living our purpose. Delving deeper, the manner of Nachiket's relationships with key people in his life seemed to have also contributed to the onset of his condition. Given the cathartic and emotional release in his meeting with Dharmaraj, Nachiket evidently felt disturbed by certain aspects in his relationships. He was young, and the tendency of the immature to both mess around and/or idealise their relationship can take an emotional toll. Often, schizophrenia is precipitated in a sensitive person by the feeling that his relationships are being threatened by others, or that they are immoral. Conflicting social ideas on matrimony and confusion on what is a permitted sexual relationship may affect the psyche at its core.

✳ ✳ ✳

John and Mary Gribben, co-authors of the book, *The One Percent Advantage,* cited earlier, have also suggested an evolutionary basis for having two distinct sexes. Consider the primordial 'ooze' of amino acids and such other life-giving material that existed at one stage in the history of the planet. An active, small cell will be able to swim around rapidly in the primordial ooze and find a partner. Such a cell will not carry much 'resources' to nurse the next generation because of its size. A big, fat cell will be an excellent provider of resources, but will not be very mobile. When small cells meet and mate, other microbes may gobble up their even smaller offspring. Big, sedentary cells will not find a mate unless a small, mobile cell swims up to them. Immediately we have the beginnings of a robust system of reproduction involving two sexes. A 'female' that provides the large egg, and a 'male' contribution that is a packet of genetic information and map for the biological development of the life-form.

The human life form is complex and a single sex with a long gestation period would have been incapable of propagating and evolving rapidly. Therefore, another component that is unrestricted from propagating during the gestation period is required. This component should also have the capability to produce offspring that can be both resource-providing components and mobile components. That is, one sex should have to have the capability to produce both sexes by passing the gene determining sex, and further, should be without impediments to mate during gestation. *Voila*—we have the male and female of the species. The evolutionary logistics of the complex human life form demanded two sexes. Nature provided this, equipping each sex with specific roles in propagation. There are two roles in biology, but one mission as a species.

Also consider that sexual intimacy (and rape, on the other extreme), as opposed to recreational sex, automatically carries with it some emotional angles. It is a sharing (or breaching) of trust that transgresses the boundaries of privacy. Hence, we are right in unequivocally condemning those who look for relationships that contravene a sense of civility (such as paedophiles). Such transgressions are in fact a failure of a human being to acknowledge one's advanced evolution. This is a failure to recognise that human beings are different from other organisms in nature by way of language and laws. It is also a failure to adopt the simple, intelligently understood need to nurture creation. We can permit ourselves instead to play out our choices without guilt, when our actions are constructive and caring, and not based on destructive lust.

*Sexual Dimorphism*, such as difference in height between sexes, is an aspect in many species. In many species, the greater size of the male correlates with the number of females that are commonly in the male's harem; that is, the bigger the male is on average in comparison with the female of the species, the more the number of females, on average, in the male's harem. In species that are monogamous, such as most birds, there is very less or no difference in size at all. The continuing difference in size between men and women hence suggests a natural tendency towards polygyny in us. There seems to be enough savage residues in us that can test our commitment to

> For now, matrimonial security (monogamy included) is still a necessity, whatever the state of civilised society in the future.

monogamous human relationships. Perhaps we will one day evolve to a point where this issue is superfluous. For now, matrimonial security (monogamy included) is still a necessity, whatever the state of civilised society in the future. The last I heard, it was still popular!

✳ ✳ ✳

The delegation of genders to distinct social roles is also the cause of much discrimination and warring. It is essential that we go beyond traditional gender roles in this advanced age. We need to accept that two sexes exist originally because of a biological need. Relationships need to be freed of gender-based jockeying for position. There is no need to prove one gender mightier than the other. This understanding helps clear the air. We must forget the skirmish of the sexes. Social roles today have enough proof that both genders have a common mission. Having said this, it is important nonetheless that we are comfortable in our sexual orientation or in relationships outside of accepted norms.

Examples of non-traditional relationships are marriages with wide age differentials, or relationships in which the women are significantly older. They could also be same-gender or inter-religious marriages (and any others that still lack common social acceptance). In this age, those who dare being in relationships that lack popular social approval had better be impervious to criticism. Perhaps times will change, but non-traditional relationships presently require great emotional maturity. Our society today, continues to test such relationships, by refusing acknowledgement. Intellectual and emotional acceptance of the relationship by the individuals in it is vital for such partnerships to succeed. Whatever the type of relationship, it is the commitment, caring and compassion shared between the members that determines its success. Any relationship that does not transgress civility and has these qualities seems valid.

Several social thinkers and lawmakers, barring a few, have advised marriage to prevent emotional rupture between members. The need for an institution of marriage, for law to support love, is a social construct to provide some security to relationships. Since wealth and its ownership are in the domain of law, it seems wise for both parties to take the shelter provided by this social construct. But, speaking with a liberal bent of mind, there really is no need for a stamp of legal validity for one-on-one relationships to succeed. We need not feel guilty just because the law has the power to declare a relationship as improper.

A relationship is always dynamic. It is an entity in motion. Hence, we need to maintain every relationship. A relationship can be likened to a virtual tank with a leak. We need to keep filling it up with nurturing thoughts, words and deeds[47]. When a deep personal intent to belong supports the relationship, maintaining it is a welcome task. If we choose to be in or out of a relationship, the decision endures successfully. The intent to belong in a relationship drives us invariably to do the right things in

---

[47]    For further insights on relations between men and women, please read the classic by GRAY, JOHN. *Men Are from Mars, Women Are from Venus*: HarperCollins publishers, 1993.

it. We must consciously invest in our relationship, learn to develop trust, and let the intent to belong in it fuel its success. When we back up our relationship with the strength of commitment, the rest will follow.

A famous personality once said anonymously, 'I would rather be single [or in a relationship] for the right reasons, than be with someone [or single] for the wrong ones.' Yet another quip, this one attributed to Socrates, is probably the last word on relationships. Despite its pessimism, it is enlightening, and seems applicable to all close personal relationships of this age, [with some modifications]: 'As to marriage [read: being in a relationship] or celibacy [read: being single], let a man [read: a person] take which course he [or she] will; he [or she] will be sure to repent it [every once in a while!]'

There is learning hidden in our emotional relationships, which although, is a learning that nobody consciously seeks. The learning from grief is virtually inevitable for all of us, while the learning that comes from heartbreak is also common enough to merit addressing. Nachiket's feelings of loss weighed heavily on him and even compounded his illness. Sometimes we have time to prepare for our losses, but sometimes the triggering event, such as sudden death, is shattering. Richard Bach in his book, *Illusions,* says, 'Here is a test to find whether your mission on earth is finished: If you're alive, it isn't.'[48] This is probably the best consolation we

---

[48]  Richard Bach in *Illusions – Adventures of a Reluctant Messiah* Dell Publishing Co., Inc. Publication (1977)

can get for the death of others, (which is usually more devastating than our own!) The next GLP for you to visit, Beginning to Start Over, looks at grief and heartbreak.

## *Section Highlights:*

- Confusion on roles and relationships often block the discovery of personal purpose and cause the onset of unwelcome thoughts of guilt and immorality.
- Feelings of distrust, jealousy and guilt can be overcome by investing effort, caring and commitment into our relationships.
- Both sexes are an evolutionary need of the species, and both genders have a common mission, so there is no need for either to jockey for superiority.
- Monogamy and matrimony are important human social constructs to promote trust and prevent emotional rupture in relationships. We may require such constructs so that law can support love.
- Any relationship between adults can endure without a formal stamp of approval from any third party if it is humane, and does not transgress civility.

# PART V: The Conclusion

The boy's results in the academic admission tests were about average. He says, 'I knew this would happen, but is there a reason?'

The mentor explained, 'You have to understand that if you practise and work at it long enough and hard enough, you will do better. You have to want it fiercely.'

The boy asks, 'How does this test judge that?'

'Well,' the mentor ventured, 'If you'd really wanted to do well in it bad enough, you would have worked hard for it.'

The boy smiles, 'So the test judged how much doing well in it meant to me.'

'Within reason… It may also have tested how long you wanted to achieve success in it,' says the mentor.

'Whoa! Does that mean if I don't get around to wanting anything I desire well in time, it won't amount to much?' was the boy's wry question.

The mentor laughed, 'Yep, it is important to move on once you realise this. We shouldn't keep trying the same old keys on the same old doors repeatedly. It will come to naught. By looking beyond past failures, you can be open to fresh chances for achievement and success. Still, not all things in life are for one to achieve or succeed in. Some are only for one to appreciate and admire. Distinguish between the two and enjoy both!'

*Anon*

# 11

# ARMOUR

r Dharmaraj briefed a counsellor on Nachiket's case and condition. Even after coming to terms with his disability, Nachiket may habitually conjure harmful and discouraging thoughts. The counsellor would provide him with some techniques to neutralise negative thinking... the harmful and unhelpful kind of thinking.

After going through his background and his present condition, the counsellor continued her discussion with Nachiket. 'Dr Dharmaraj told me to help you with overcoming unhelpful thoughts. Are such thoughts triggered by memories?'

Nachiket replied, 'Not strictly memories. Often they are due to some judgments... my own and those of others.'

'Flawed thoughts come from certain habits we pick up early,' the counsellor explained. 'The point then is to change the habits. Recognise that these thinking patterns are not helpful and challenge them. There is a systematic methodology to change this, which I will teach you. Positive, but realistic self-talk and the steps we will discuss are often all that is needed. You can break bad thinking habits and build new habits that will foster confidence.'

Over the course of the next few meetings, the counsellor walked Nachiket through the steps for handling random discouraging thoughts[50]. Once Nachiket got a hang of the technique, the counsellor asked, 'Do you have any doubts?'

Nachiket was keen on getting his life back in order, and countered, 'Do I need to know anything else to get started?'

The counsellor answered. 'Life is meant for you to do, learn and enjoy. You will experience several unique incidents as you go on, some of which may test your limits. Don't get disheartened. You will learn everything you need from them. The learning never stops. Learn from life and look beyond every setback. Your life will then in turn be progressive and rewarding. The thing to understand is that emotions depend on thoughts. Change the thought and you change the emotion. It needs some effort, but the technique really helps. If you keep applying it consciously, you can overcome the habit of thinking adversely,' reassured the counsellor.

'Does this mean I can pursue a normal life? You know: education, work, marriage, children...?' inquired Nachiket.

---

[50]     See GLP 6, The Last Error, in the Good Living Practices section at the end of the book

'I would say yes,' declared the counsellor. 'There are certain things you learn only on the job, so to speak. I think the foundation is set and you can venture to bigger challenges.'

After the last meeting with the counsellor, she watched Nachiket as he walked away with a definite spring in his step. Nachiket turned back and flashed a thumbs-up sign. The counsellor smiled and returned the sign.

Nachiket no longer felt discouraged when things did not go his way, and always picked himself up. He spoke affirmations to himself. He continually made the effort to challenge reactive negative thoughts and replace them with helpful proactive thinking. The words 'Change the thought, change the emotion' had charged Nachiket.

When the sessions with Dr Dharmaraj and the counsellor concluded Nachiket felt as much in control as anyone normally would. He returned to his disrupted academics and began working towards his goals in earnest. He felt the thrill of using his mind and achieving goals that he set for himself. His unique learning had provided a progressive perspective, a 'can-do' attitude and an unshakeable belief in *grace*. Nachiket just knew there was no need to puzzle over whether such a grace was divine or mundane.

## FINAL ENABLERS

Getting that new car, acquiring a university degree and the like are all valid goals. However, it is personal purpose, which keeps us motivated to achieve our goals in a special and unique manner. When we travel our personal purpose, we enjoy the achievement of the goals we choose, and look for new ones constantly, overcoming any fatigue, failure or frustration. In these last few sections of the book, we converge on the final elements of a mindset that makes such a personal purpose easier to recognise and apply. It outlines some ideas that can help the afflicted or the diffident, come back and operate in the social mainstream.

In this demanding world, it is inevitable that we experience testing interactions with others and the environment. We need to have certain skills and attitudes for being constructive in our interactions. A book is never a replacement for practise, but the following paragraphs discuss some factors important for interacting in and with our world. These ideas can enhance our ability to function effectively in our personal and professional environments.

## EMPATHY:

An important aid in interaction is empathy. The push for empathy has become quite a cliché. Of course, clichés become clichés because they have some truth. When appropriately practised, empathy works to build bridges between people, except when it comes to the die-hard and opinionated. Nevertheless, before we conclude that we have tried and failed, even with such people, empathy deserves full consideration. A villain too may have very good reasons to be villainous. Empathy, as you know, is seeing things from the other person's point of view. The definition is easy enough, but implementing it is another story. So how do we empathise? Here are some pointers.

The first step towards empathising is to respect the fact that others have independent wishes, ideas, and needs, though we may not subscribe to them. That is, we appreciate that different backgrounds lead to different understanding. Instead of feeling outright contempt, anger, or any other disturbing sentiment, we first need to acknowledge the whole person. Once this stage is set, it is easier to focus on the real issue of our disagreement instead of personality related issues. When you are able to recognise and appreciate that you are unique, it will be a small step to acknowledge that others are too.

> The first step towards empathising is to respect the fact that others have independent wishes, ideas, and needs, though we may not subscribe to them.

Next, it is important to listen. Often, when we let the other person have their FULL say, a different picture emerges and we can see reasons for people to feel the way they feel. In fact, they themselves would realise the flaws in their reasoning or emotions if any, when you provide them with supportive listening. If instead, we attack, or attempt rationality, before hearing people out, they may become defensive, or hostile.

Further, *we* can do some things to make the other person be open and more empathetic while we practise empathy. First, communicate directly, but in a manner that avoids pointing fingers at their personality. Avoid crass phrases such as, 'Your careless attitude makes me angry,' or 'I hate it when you act cool.' Personality could be in-built. What matters is how people are contributing to the circumstances and context. You can point to that, but not at personality. Second, avoid rhetorical questions. For example—'Why are you so forgetful?' or 'Why are you always late?' There are no answers to such questions. Instead, hear the person out as is relevant to the context. Third, establish that you are trying to understand. The best thing is to be explicit about this by saying things like 'I am trying to understand, but I am confused,' or 'What you say will make more sense to me if you explain a little more.' The other person's emotional approach will be defused. They may try a different angle that could help resolve the issue.

Empathy includes the ability to respect the priorities of others. People see you as part of a solution when they realise that you are putting effort aligned towards a common result. People will be willing to build on your effort, contribute to any work-in-process and help in its completion. Your individual actions carry you towards your goals in the wake of a common result.

Finally, in any effort, personal or professional, if *you* haven't figured out what you are doing, nobody will. You control this aspect of empathy. Hence, make sure you thoroughly understand what you want to accomplish. Seek information that can help you understand. When you understand what you are trying to offer, your communication will be lucid. Others will be disposed to accept it. You do not need to travel the whole distance for a sense of clarity. Like driving a car with headlights, be clear about what is in your immediate vision. You will then travel the whole way, a little at a time.

When we practise empathy, we may think, *Why should I try so hard when the other person is being difficult?* We could have already set up some expectations for the result of empathising. We feel some *quid pro quo* is in order. In our minds, we are transacting with empathy instead of using it to improve communication. We should refrain from treating empathy as a currency of exchange. We have to view this as a selfless contribution. If it helps, well and good. If it does not, don't let it affect you. Come away with your dignity intact.

A last thought on empathising. When an individual passionately subscribes to an idea, although it is patently wrong, you probably have no chance of persuading the person. In such instances, the best thing to do may be to use an external influencer, walk away until a better time or wait till the person discovers their folly on their own. Sometimes it is the most empathetic thing to do.

## DECISIONS:

Most choices we have to make are not as dire as deciding which of the twins gets a seat in the lifeboat. Agreed, most of us have faced tough choices that could have led to regret. Should I send that money for father's medication or pay my mounting credit card debt? Do I put my aged dog to sleep, or continue to take care of her until she dies naturally? Do I risk being a little unprepared for my meeting early tomorrow and help my son with his math quiz, or lose sleep to prepare for the meeting and risk being a little unfocused? It seems obvious that something has to give.

When there has to be a sacrifice on the one part to opt for the other, it makes us feel terrible. Most decisions, however, are much simpler than a seat in a lifeboat. You can get away with few regrets, whatever the consequence. However, every once in a while, along comes a situation about which you have insufficient information. You know that some decisions are leaps of faith that you could regret later on. How do you choose and unequivocally accept that choice for the long run?

There may be several things to regret. For instance, you could regret not being a doctor, a journalist, or a movie star. You could regret not having been

> The more you focus on what you have now the more you focus on your learning (or growth).

prudent and saved for a house. You could have regrets on matters that relate to saving a life. You may ponder that you could have saved your reputation if you had been more sincere. Whatever the regrets may be, we must realise that mistakes and puzzles of the past can help us act proactively now. Experience is the way you use yesterday. You know that rationally, but you also have to trust time to heal the impact of a wrong decision emotionally. The more you focus on the sacrifice (or mistake), the more you focus on loss. The more you focus on what you have now, the more you focus on your learning (or growth).

It helps to have a firm belief that all the choices you made, before this point, have facilitated your learning. What you have is the raw material with which you can build. When you use your experience, you are aware of the *you* that has taken shape—the person you are today. Be true to that person. Use your experience instead of reliving your past. Avoid old addictions or going back to behaviours that you know have harmed you.

We are left with the decision of taking one twin on the lifeboat. What can you say to that person making the decision? Very little as regards the image of the other twin on the burning deck. Let go, you made a difficult decision. Let go of the loss. Forgive the errors even if you cannot forget. Next time, plan to have extra lifeboats and carry extra  life jackets, just in case.

## VEXATIONS:

The comfort you feel with your decisions and choices will invariably be disturbed. Genuine arguments and disagreements do not cause this disturbance. These usually have rational resolutions. Real vexations are from the subtle ridicule, unfair arm-twisting, or other forms of power-play that sometimes occur in social interactions. For some, these power plays are a way of life. They move on, inexorably trampling sentiment, decency and dignity. They may be blissfully unaware that they have compromised the self-esteem, or triggered discontent, in another human being. Ordinarily, any good boss, team player, or other interfacing party will try to build upon the interaction to progress. However, the vexatious class, jockeys for superiority instead, and uses various psychological ploys to denigrate others' contributions.

We can only make guesses as to why some individuals behave in a vexatious manner. Their position is tenuous without props; they suffer from a sense of inadequacy, or, they have ambitions built on relative worth. You cannot address most of the reasons why, so do not try to change these individuals. It will only add to your vexation. Typically, they have deep-set, inflexible convictions about the way the world is, and our attempts at being reasonable may not change their approach.

A common trait of vexatious people is that they change their stand frequently and unreliably. Vexatious individuals also often resort to aggressive or sarcastic criticism to undermine others. Sometimes, such a person may withhold key facts to deliberately scuttle your declarations; declarations that you would not have made had you known the facts earlier. Alternatively, they could hijack an interaction convened for a specific purpose and steer it to a personal agenda. Vexatious individuals, usually, regard themselves as the only thing that matters, excluding everything else.

Pressures in interactions, which attempt to force a bias, are political realities that we cannot ignore. They are a part of any collaborative entity, such as families, corporations and governments. Please understand that you cannot change this. We cannot always react to put-downs, verbal-jousting or psychological ploys used by some people. Sometimes, you could feel that to react would transgress the bounds of protocol. You may think you cannot afford to antagonise such people, but most likely, they are in conflict with a larger whole in their philosophy already. We must therefore learn to manage the vexations we face in interactions. We can read the signs and take steps to be poised.

Firstly, the most important factor to handle vexatious people is being sure you are right. This breed can sense uncertainty like a dog can sense fear. Once they know you are unsure, out comes a steamroller of heavy-handed statements. Hence, before you take up an issue with this group of people, be sure you are right and that you have lined up all your ducks. Do your homework.

Second, it is useful to remember the recent history of your interactions with them. They generally take advantage of the forgetfulness of others. They may confuse, contort, and lie without tangible proof of their earlier assurances. You will have to make a conscious effort to remember and record your interactions if you want to make progress with this breed. This means, ever so often during the interaction, sum up and restate the facts so that they are obvious to all concerned. A firm restatement of your position, its relation to the context, and how it is relevant in the present, will help you make headway.

Finally, be detached from the issue or any of its aspects. People attached to an issue focus on defending their turf instead of a larger relevant agenda. They are likely to be reactive instead of proactive. Emotional attachment can make us miss some salient points. Your passion has its place, but it cannot replace your presence of mind. Be in the moment. Concentrate on the context.

# ANGER:

A brief exploration of the emotion of anger may help us understand its adverse effects while also highlighting why it is sometimes valid. Anger is often a by-product of envy, jealousy and relative measurement. These aspects, or a breach of trust, or being annoyed, or a sense of helplessness and lack of control, may trigger anger. Anger erupts when we are at the receiving end of someone else's unacceptable attitude or behaviour. It germinates from attacks on our sensibility and from our discomfort with someone else's airs, habits, or beliefs. These instigate an instinctive unease. Being excessively attached emotionally is at the root.

We are likely to lose our temper when others push our buttons, deliberately or otherwise. Like envy, it does not come from disagreement with an idea or event. We are patient with those we like, even in disagreement. It's debatable, but anger is often personal. There is something in the individual triggering anger that we cannot tolerate. Anger usually, cannot result from a rational process of disagreement. Most people only work out the cause later on, after they have blown their cool.

Nonetheless, not all anger is bad. Losing your temper can be good in some situations. People tell you it is bad to lose your temper. They gloss over the portion that losing your temper is bad only when you lose it without controlling the emotion. When you lose control, the damage you can cause is sometimes irreparable. You say and do things that you may regret later on. However, losing your temper can be good when it is a conscious release. When you base your indignation or frustration on facts, and when the situation can do with escalation, it could be wise to display your temper. It can be a valid response to unjust, flagrant or aggressive transgressions—wrongdoings that invite no debate as to their illegitimacy.

When people tell you to control your temper, never confuse it with valid anger. What is bad is to lose control and flail out wildly with words and actions that are destructive. When you use it with care, anger can be a powerful ally to call upon in times of conflict. The knack is to make sure you are in control, channelling all the energy from the emotion. It also prevents you from bottling up a valid reaction and adopting a timid attitude when you are the victim. Focus on the context of the disagreement when there is one, and seek a rational resolution. Decline the use of the surrogate sense, and any need to respond recklessly to spurious stimuli. You have the knowledge to be proactive. You can choose to get angry when anger is appropriate.

## COOPERATIVE RECIPROCITY:

Cooperative reciprocity, as explored before, is a survival strategy based on Dr Robert Trivers work about the evolution of cooperation in a species[51]. In lay terms, it suggests doing exactly what the 'other person' does,

---

[51] Dr Robert Trivers, as cited earlier, is currently a Professor of Anthropology and Biological Sciences at Rutgers University, USA. The practical applications suggested here are the author's interpretation and not the views of Dr Trivers.

positive or negative, after offering cooperation in the beginning or commencement of the interaction. Cooperative reciprocity works in most cases. It is a practical survival strategy.

How does cooperative reciprocity work? Be nice if they are nice. Do not be nice if they are not nice. This simple technique pays huge dividends. This means whenever you approach anyone on the first instance with an issue, extend a hand of cooperation, then respond exactly as they act from that point on. If they raise their voice, raise yours. If they use an obscene word, use one. If they ignore you, ignore them. However, if they move one step in your direction, move one step in theirs. If they use a conciliatory tone, do the same. If they alternate between cooperative and hostile positions, do the same, close on the heels of their action. Try it.

Extend cooperation on the first or perhaps the second instance of every interaction, despite any adverse move. Then do exactly as the person has done to you, but in a manner that makes it clear, you are for the larger agenda. This means that while you may get personal in an interaction, you should concurrently convey your focus on the larger progressive and common agenda. The art of cooperative reciprocity lies in picking the pivotal factor in the unconstructive act or words and retorting with something similar. Focus on the context and retort constructively.

The next time you face negativity, pick the pivotal discomfiting factor (such as a gesture, a phrase, a tone, etc.) and think up a creative counter using that same trait (or the opposite of it), while sticking to the larger context. The key is to pick what you instinctively feel is the transgression and retort. A simple example, if the other person just yelled, you can contrast powerfully by replying with a firm, steady tone. Extend cooperation once or twice more, *before* you yell back. If the person is acting like a jerk, you can contrast it by laughing. And, of course, you CAN get angry without losing control to the emotion.

You may be able to use cooperative reciprocity in any interaction, but with these caveats.

Caveat#1: Modify the intensity of reciprocation to suit the protocol of the situation. For example, the way to interact one-on-one may not be the same as in the presence of a third-party.

Caveat#2: Offer out-of-the-way cooperation only when you are in an enduring relationship. Such exceptional cooperation pays off only with continuing opportunities of interactions in the future.

Caveat#3: Don't forsake extending cooperation, care or compassion for the ones who deserve it, despite interactions that are rare or one-time.

In general, you should either get even with, or avoid, undeserving *gross* and *subtle* cheaters. Gross cheaters are the ones who never cooperate or return a favour. Subtle cheaters are the ones who do seem to be cooperating, but gradually lessen it, and then let you down. You should consciously hold off or taper your cooperation in such cases. When you have interacted often enough or with sufficient involvement, you will be able to distinguish the undeserving cheaters from the fair players.

# DIFFICULTIES:

When you hit a low, and you feel none of your work is bearing fruit, when you feel you are unable to make any more effort, be patient. The tide will turn. It is the rule of the cosmos that things move in cycles. There are things you can never understand, and it is best to bide your time. Acknowledging this human fate is difficult. The mind does feel frustrated at such times, and it seeks a way out, hammering against the rock-solid walls of circumstance and inner limitations. You can hammer away, but you will only hurt yourself more. The natural cycle of life will instead cradle you and lift you with the passage of time. When you recognise this, you realise that nothing about your moods or situation is permanent. There will be times when you are feeling good and others when you feel low. Meanwhile, be patient.

Funnel any disturbing energy in you into a creative pursuit. Write a letter to yourself or to some other individual to whom you feel you have to express yourself. Do not post it, but merely let out your feelings. If you have no one to write to, write to whatever power you believe in. A sense of hopelessness in our low times may lock-in some of us. The mere act of writing can relieve us, and provide hope. Have faith that someone is listening. In fact, someone always is— your subconscious. It will work in mysterious ways to dissipate harmful energies and provide a new course and direction to you. Once you have done this letter writing, you will be in a clearer frame of mind. Now you are ready to stake your claim on the things you need to get out of the situation. Meanwhile, be patient.

Often, we just fail to ask. We forget that the squeaky wheel gets the grease. After thinking over and framing your requirements, approach those who can help. Refuse to let the box limit you. Help is available, professionally and personally. Sometimes just visits to the library or a little time spent browsing on the Internet would help you locate the assistance you need. At this stage, sow as many seeds as possible. Some will grow into saplings. Nurture the ones that grow carefully, as any of them could bear fruit. Meanwhile, be patient.

✳ ✳ ✳

Both the ups and the downs in life pass helpful learning on to us. It is hard when the downs are great adversities or prolonged states of sadness. When this happens, trust time. It will give you your learning appropriately. It might come to you in disguise. When we are looking for physical comfort, we could get emotional growth. When we look for emotional solace, we may find an intellectual treasure; or when we are looking for wisdom…we find love.

Be open to learn *whatever the past teaches*; and surely, you will grow. Believe there is betterment *of some kind* from this point forward, and surely, you will find it. Be ready to receive abundance *in any form*, and surely, you will have it. When you feel hopeless, recognise that this will also pass and that some learning will be gained from it.

This might seem like an exercise in faith. However, if you trust time—betterment and wellness will become evident. It may be under several layers, but you can realise there are some things to be grateful for, whatever your circumstances. You could be grateful that you are whole in limb, that your relationships are supportive, that you ate yesterday, that you still sleep, that you are sane, and so on. There are reasons to be grateful today, however dissatisfying your past has been, and however distant your dreams may seem.

> There are reasons to be grateful today, however dissatisfying your past has been, and however distant your dreams may seem.

✳ ✳ ✳

If harsh events mark your past, it may hamper your thinking progressively. You have to come to the present and treat the rest as fated. You have to work on caring for yourself. Once you genuinely love life, no one and nothing can disturb your comfort. The last GLP to visit is The Last Error. This GLP will help you handle disturbing and unhelpful thoughts. You may have such thoughts just out of habit, despite having understood personal purpose.

## *Section Highlights:*

- Acquiring the ability to empathise is an important enabler for achievement.
- Focus on what you have, instead of what is lost, for a better life.
- We need to handle people who are vexations to the spirit by being sufficiently detached and contextual.

- Anger may be a valid response when we are victims of unfair behaviour or judgements. However, one should be in control of the emotion and use it wisely.
- *Cooperative reciprocity* can be practically applied by being aware and detached, while retaining the option to walk away from deadlocked situations.
- When nothing is going your way, be patient and as receptive of change as you can be. Trust time to cradle you in its natural cycle.
- Just try and you can end up loving life.

# 12

# RESOLUTION

*(A peek into Nachiket's later ramblings)*

**I** have come a long way from believing I am a mythological persona. Now, I am trying to be rational. What I have to say might be hard to digest. Many claim the ultimate refuge for us is religion. But, many people today seem to adopt religion to escape or because they are superstitious and afraid to be without its support. They are often not practitioners by faithful independent choice. Some even follow religion because they have a fanatical belief of a return to the 'glory' days—a time when their religion was undisputable. The moderate few are also emotionally inclined towards faith rather than persuaded by rationality. Religion provides emotional solace, but very thin logic. When one thinks about it, misinterpreted religion has divided societies and been the basis for several uncivilised acts. We cannot rely on any single template that declares what is required, because a single template cannot celebrate all beliefs in our world. In actuality, religion might need modulating by civilised reason.

What is the promise of religion that people realise when they practise it? The purpose of a spiritual life, many believe, is self-realisation. Godhead, Heaven, or Enlightenment is commonly claimed as our ultimate goal. Religion claims one can achieve a state of perfection, or some ultimate state. A vast plethora of gurus and religious leaders provide analyses of complex holy texts towards this end. These 'teachers' tend to din it into you that you have something lacking that can be filled only by the divine. Their clarifications of the ultimate goal are at best perfunctory and poetic, because they are trying to describe a sensation of ultimate divinity, beyond life. If you are a lover of verse, the beauty of these words may leave you spellbound. It can make you thirst for a state of perfection with unsurpassed fervour. All the while, this is reinforcing the idea that what you are is not enough.

An omniscient transcendental wisdom, or some all-encompassing abstract yet tangible collection of human wisdom as some perceive in a supposedly realised soul, could be a myth or legend. If we delve into this mystery, one will soon realise its limitations. The knowledge base within reach of humanity exists in isolated pockets of understanding. It is incapable of revealing an underlying commonality, if such commonality exists at all. Contemplating and pushing ourselves to experience enlightenment and any eventual divine destination can be psychologically dangerous. There are several paradoxes in religion. Trying logic on these paradoxes often leads to a dead-end. Too much introspection may trigger psychological side-effects or mental disabilities, and hamper effective functioning in everyday life.

Nirvana, Godhead, Self-realisation, or Heaven, by its very definition, is impractical. The mind is capable of conceiving and describing these states poetically; but it cannot experience the states in its current limited form. Since by definition such an experience would have to be all-encompassing, there would be no palpable direction even if we end up in it. There would be no further goals or measures when such states are achieved. The experience hence lacks any sense of purpose and direction. We cannot begin to understand these states within our lifetime, even if they exist, as we just do not have the physiological or mental infrastructure. We may not act in sync with reality if we implode into potentially detached, all-encompassing, and yet null states. It is impossible to grasp an all-knowing, everlasting, all-pervading unity within the confines of our given senses. We would go mad.

Are such states just a rosy promise? Is it pointless and wishful then? 'Living happily' can be real when we debunk any obsession with Nirvana, Heaven and such endpoints, and go about living with any faith or attitude that is caring and compassionate. What I now understand is that we may decay and disintegrate in social goals if we forsake the immediate here and now for that which is outside the experienced. To belong and feel motivated, our goals have to be tangible and real. To be here, now in the present, we need to scale down any huge spiritual end-game and go about pursuing definite, real, and personal goals for ourselves and our world instead. What we are is enough for our 'real' world. Get concerned with it. Come to the present, the here and now, and solve immediate human problems. Pay attention to 'real' problems (and 'God' knows, there are several).

Despite all I have read, I should not look for a state of all pervading omniscience and everlasting bliss. All pervading and everlasting happiness, completeness and consciousness, if they do exist at all, are not teachable or acquirable using our current faculties simply because they are without measure. If it exists, the experience probably happens by *grace*. I can only pray for that grace—physical, emotional, intellectual and spiritual, to enter my experience. For me, the Big One can wait (or should I say, I can wait for the Big One).

Nachiket

## CLARITY IN CONTROL

Control. How much people desire control! Control over the work they do and its results, their desires, their relationships, and their living in general. Our balance, poise, positive sense, and our ability to be proactive all seem to depend on the extent of our being in control. Of course, things do not always go as planned. Murphy's Law crops up in several of our activities. Why is it difficult to be calm and proactive when faced with challenges to our sense of control? What is the ideal outlook that can keep us worry-free? We need to understand that happy medium of existence where we can manage our degree of control without anxiety. The final ideas in the book are about how to set fresh terms in our world.

Think of our responses in any situation as resulting from the overlapping of three virtual spheres. The three spheres are the individual's circles of influence, concern, and dependence (Pic. 4—Spheres in our Decision Space). We take decisions and respond based on the sphere that for us is the largest for the situation. If pressures of social protocol from our being dependent, forces our hand, we make compromises. When our concerns involve things we cannot do anything about, we feel frustrated. In addition, if we cannot influence the things we feel we should be able to, we may feel inadequate. We cannot do away with the spheres that affect our sense of poise, but we can learn how to manage them.

Pic 4. Spheres in our Decision Space

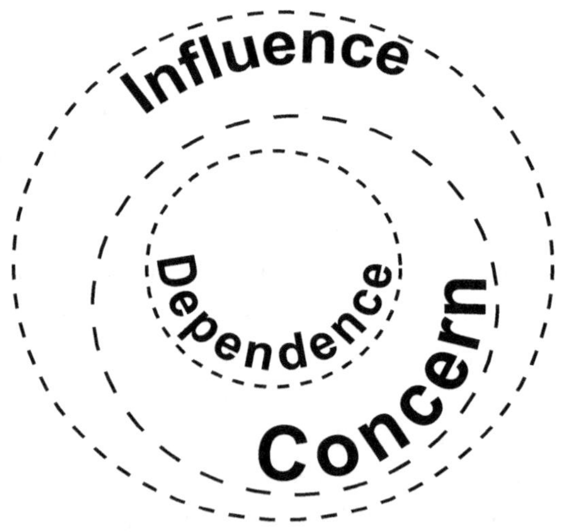


It will be obvious that we have to shrink the sphere of our dependence to the greatest possible degree.

When you exhaust the transient props that support you and replace them, to the extent possible, with enduring ones, this sphere shrinks. But, it is necessary to stay concerned about a broader set of issues, than only things we depend on. This circle of concern is our source of motivation. Concern cannot manifest itself without interest, and interest cannot come without involvement. If you feel unconcerned today, become involved. Involvement is what motivates you and gets you into the mainstream.

Some view a job purely as a source of income—in which case they cannot be motivated for long. But, if we learn more about our company: its stakeholders, fellow employees, the business functions and aims, we can become involved. It is likely we will get drawn into the mainstream, as we get interested in the bigger picture. Our circle of concern should hence be of a size that includes a greater set, a set that would motivate us. However, the concern should ideally be within what we can influence.

It is exceedingly important to know what we can and cannot influence. *Whatever does not have a solution within what you can influence cannot be your problem.* Sure, you could contribute in a roundabout way, but the problem is somebody else's. How can something you cannot influence be your problem? While we know the problem is as real as one's existence, it is also a given that you can do precious little about it. Therefore, you should accept your existence 'as-is where-is' as suggested earlier, in the section, *An Atomic Association.* Accept your problems and reach out, as suggested in the section on challenge, *The Hidden Navigator.* When we are clear about what is personally possible, all unnecessary tension and anxiety would drop out of our scheme.

Anybody can stay concerned with one's life, at the very least. However, our circle of influence will be small if we look at life only in this way. How do we increase our influence in the things that concern us? How can this influence stretch beyond a concern for oneself alone? When we act on opportunities to add value to others, we invariably add value to ourselves. Adding value is the only way to increase the size of your sphere of influence. Your value addition requires some action—mental, menial or material. It requires effort. As suggested in the section, *The Bona Fide Battle,* result or value, is wholly dependent on intent. A committed intent, which aims at contributing to a larger order, will unleash the required effort. How do we develop this intent? How do we ensure relevance and continuity in value delivery and hence, influence? How do we get involved gladly? This is next.

## *Section Highlights:*

- What we can influence, what we are concerned about and what we depend on, should take a descending order in the magnitude of their impact.
- Such a sequence of impact can ensure we are without harmful anxiety and that we remain motivated.
- Whether this is consistently so or not, we should accept the situation, while trying to retain or regain balance.

- We can retain or regain balance by creating value—mental, menial or material, for others and ourselves.

## THE VALUE VENUE

The way to establish ourselves in a personally purposeful and value-creating journey is merely to begin. Create the value that contributes to betterment with small steps. With a strong intent, even the worthless or shabby can turn into something excellent. To deliver value effectively and efficiently, we need to make efforts, personalise interests of others, and take ownership of our tasks with dedication.

Effort is an aspect of value that ensures one can 'perspire' and achieve. It removes any need to be born gifted or to be a genius to get extraordinary results.

> With a strong intent, even the worthless or the shabby can turn into excellence.

Effort is old-fashioned hard work. However, we would not be calling it 'work' when it deals with what we are concerned about (our only obligations). You get to see 'work' as enjoyable. Your work translates to and becomes value, for yourself and others.

Imagine you had to fill in a database of 1,000,000 records (names and addresses, etc.). Not knowing when you would finish, you apportioned your and your team's time, and then worked doggedly for days on end. A database file that was only a fraction of a gigabyte began to grow. You got an archiving program and began backing it up on multiple media. You also made a copy on a mirrored server. You setup automatic backups and strict risk-mitigation measures as the database grew and grew. The end in mind was slowly becoming reality. Then, one morning, you uploaded the database on your client's server. You never knew (and will never know) its usage. That instant when the upload was complete, and you received the closing payment, was worth it all. How is this valuable to you, leaving the payment aside? The real question to consider is are you better in one manner or another? We usually are when we add value. In this case, you probably became more seasoned in your skills of data storage and management.

Respecting the small efforts as much as the big ones is necessary. We need *not* keep waiting for 'judgment day' to recognise what we are doing as worthwhile. Whatever you are doing is worthwhile if it is getting better and better every day *in some manner*. When we have worked hard without expecting miracles, every joy is multi-fold because the moment of achievement then *just happens*. A number of negligible small acts would magically transform into a worthy result. In the humility of the doer to take small steps lies the ability to achieve big results. Respect the littlest effort, wasted or otherwise, and a payoff is inevitable. A payoff for what you are working towards… often. A payoff for yourself… always! For remember, our abilities, knowledge and wisdom keeps growing.

This brings us to the second driver for effectiveness after the important ingredient of effort. You must personalise. Think of personalisation as a selfless effort for personal betterment. This seeming contradiction can be a revelation. It is about letting go the minor ego for a bigger self. Personalisation means: To have a personal yet broad empathetic perspective. This cannot happen unless you practise being inclusive. We have already discussed empathy, but its importance cannot be understated. Empathise with your spouse and kids and you have a happy family. Empathise with your boss and customers and you have a great job. Empathise with the community and the world at large and you become an involved citizen.

The final driver to delivering value, after effort and personalisation, is that of our sense of ownership. This refers to a sense of belonging to our chosen process. Ownership involves respect on an institutional scale. We cannot truly belong to something we disrespect. Whether it is a job or a relationship, you can do more by respecting it. Ownership happens with symbiosis between the individual and the *process*. There is a two-way flow of value between the person and the process of achievement. This symbiotic relationship will ensure learning or some other gain for you, tangible or intangible, while the process goes towards a specific result: personal, professional or social.

As I tried to reinforce, many times over, in assorted places in the book, you will find you can achieve more when you dedicate yourself to something larger. When you wholeheartedly choose to serve something larger in time, place and perspective, you will unleash an unmatched drive. Whatever the current circumstance, be assured you will grow into being proactive and confident if you accept your state and deliver value, even a little at a time.

✳ ✳ ✳

These concluding thoughts on control and value should get you up and running with your personal purpose. If you feel you still cannot do this effectively in your situation, you may need to arm yourselves with new goals that can help in a two-way flow of value between you and what concerns you. *If we have no options to change things, it might be time to develop a respect, beyond acceptance, for our condition. It is not a problem. It is the truth.* If you seek change or want to bring about change, search and choose what you can respect. Choose wisely.

*<u>Section Highlights:</u>*

- With focused effort, we can ensure value creation.
- When we personalise and have empathy, our focus grows sharper. We understand what value to deliver. Clearly.
- A sense of ownership for the venues where we deliver value lends motivation, drives effort and leads to satisfying and worthwhile results.
- If we cannot respect our current situation enough to feel motivated, we need to search and choose that which can command our respect.

## BEING HERE NOW

You should be able to link the ideas presented so far with three concepts, which the book offers as its keystones. The crux of the personal success the book expounds is in understanding and applying this triad. We devoted a large part to discussing ideas and attitudes to do just that. Once grasped, these 'mantras' enable a personal acceptance of existence and its purpose. The three 'mantras' are,

1.  Meet your fate; make your destiny.
2.  Realise your absolute, non-relative and unique standing.
3.  Know [your] betterment in every circumstance.

The first of the triad *Meet your fate; make your destiny*, reflects an attitude that helps us accept our state of affairs while maintaining control. We can interpret fate as what we meet and destiny as how we meet it. There is no way out if we remain in a state of denial or apathy. Instead, embrace the here and now. This is accepting fate. Taking control requires a firm resolve to be at the centre of your life and to be a value creator. That's how you carve your destiny. It is never too late. Do not question your fate. Act on your destiny. If you understand the ideas and apply the basic set of tools provided, you will progress.

The second part of the triad, *Realise your absolute, non-relative and unique standing*, is an attitude that drops jealousy, envy and the blame-game. Your standing is unrelated to any pecking order. Granted, social structures have a purpose in the management of civilised life and make some demands on you purely for the sake of protocol. However, these demands can be easily accepted by if, at your core, you realise what a unique creation *you* are, as is *everybody* else. Be proud of what you are and what you achieve. Be anchored in the uniqueness that is YOU.

---

**BILL OF RIGHTS**

- I have the right to say No without feeling guilty
- I have the right to do what will make me happy, as long as it does not infringe on another person's rights
- I have the right to ask for help
- I have the right to feel angry
- I have the right to feel confused
- I have the right not to care [worry]
- I have the right to offer no excuses for my behaviour
- I have the right to have my needs respected
- I have the right not to know the answer
- I have the right to disagree
- I have the right to be weak
- I have the right to make a mistake and be responsible for it
- I have the right to cry
- I have the right to be scared
- I have the right not to like everybody
- I have the right to get what I pay for
- I have the right to ask for what I want, knowing that I can be refused
- I have the right to be listened to, and the right to be taken seriously
- I have the right to set my own priorities
- I have the right to change my mind
- I have the right to privacy
- I have the right to get professional help
- I have the right to be non-assertive
- I have the bodily right to walk away

The third and last part of the triad, *Know [your] betterment in every circumstance*, relates to the path of constant growth, learning and wisdom. The consequences of our actions could be positive or negative, but once we realise everything contributes to personal progress, we would take what comes our way with a degree of composure. Every instance can be seen as an opportunity to grow. In testing times, we can be detached and poised, when waiting for the tide to turn. Even in the most dismal of circumstances, if your spirit can accept and adapt, you will walk away with the confidence to face a new day. May be just a little, or, may be slowly, but you get to appreciate that things improve… may be perpetually!

Our 'Bill of Rights,' as suggested by Dr Jerilyn Ross (1946–2010), is reproduced in the box. Dr Ross was a pioneer and expert on therapies for anxiety disorders and co-author, with Rosalynn Carter, of the book *Triumph Over Fear*. This Bill of Rights is reassuring in that it tells us it is okay to be human. It seems enough to seek life, one small step at a time. You just need to get started on it. Consciously.

✳ ✳ ✳

Our psyche might need one other thing to make it complete. Many thinkers extol the power of prayer as divine grace, or in mundane terms, as a powerful suggestion to the sub-conscious. Yet several people do not pray. The reason could be we are ignorant of how to pray, or that we feel too undeserving to pray genuinely. We view the day-to-day acts we perform under the lens of self-judgment. To this self-judgment, life may add a lot of external criticism, unnecessary competition and flagrant aggression for us to face. These could leave us feeling guilty, fearful or unworthy in our attempts to relate to a greater power.

We may oscillate between fear and guilt, instead of feeling blessed, when we attempt prayer. It is tough to ask for blessings or express gratitude when we doubt ourselves. On the other hand, a lot of our conditioning regarding how to worship, confuses our love and caring for ourselves, with being selfish or as narcissistic. To pray or summon self-affirmations without a negative bias, the most important attitudes are sincerity and forgiveness. We can never pray until we give ourselves the caring, kindness and compassion we expect from the rest of the world. We can lay every discouragement or struggle at the altar of existence and accept the fact that our life is not perfect, and does not need to be so. This is humility. We can forgive our trespasses, and know that we deserve the opportunity to improve ourselves. This is self-love. Caring prayer and loving affirmations work in ways that seem almost magical; whether you believe its power is divine, as in a God, or mundane, as in a suggestion to the subconscious. Forgive, persevere and pray… sincerely.

If you have already visited the Good Living Practices (GLPs), this book ends here. If you are yet to visit the GLPs, do read and apply them. You might want to read the Epilogue as well. Use the GLPs in your toolkit and you should feel free. Life could be full of simple solutions to complex problems. People think only complex solutions work because they feel their problems are insurmountable without difficult techniques. I offered, in the book, some basic ideas and information that have helped me. They can help you develop your unique cognitive core too, which in turn will then guide you. The past, collective or individual, can no longer hold us back. Once you make the resolve to grow, all you go through, good and bad will add to your experience.

A little technique to get you started, even if you are not able to begin doing any of the GLPs, is the *five-minute promise*. All you have to do is make a promise to yourself that you will devote five minutes to a real, achievable and compelling task before you decide you cannot go on. Give the task you pick your wholehearted attention for just five minutes. If the task does not grab you and you feel apathetic, despite a pressing need to carry on, there is probably something physically wrong, and you may need professional help.

We have explored life and its strategies; now go ahead and own your life, on *your* terms. You can accept and build, right here and right now, on any moment whatsoever, wherever you are, and whatever you are. Soon, you will find that you and your existence are somewhat complete. You will not regret the past, or have to fear the future, when your *I, Me and Us* are 'being (in the) here (and the) now.'

# THE BEGINNING!

# Appendix—
# Good Living Practices (GLPs) Toolkit

# GLP 1

## FLYING ABOVE THE FLAK

*F*ear is a major factor preventing people from making progress. When people are timid about confronting challenges, they may find it hard to start. No matter how much our cognitive understanding develops, historical dogma and impulses surface frequently. There could be attempts to invade our space—physical, mental, or emotional. We may end up feeling afraid. If we react with fear, instead of confronting such attempts proactively, the fear can push us further into disturbing feelings.

This GLP helps in remaining poised when afraid. One cannot banish fear, but we can manage it. A simple six-step process for fear-control based on Dr Jerilyn Ross's original technique is included here[52]. Dr Jerilyn Ross (1946–2010), recommended these six steps in contextual

---

[52]   Ross, Jerilyn and Carter, Rosalynn: *Triumph Over Fear*; Bantam Books, 1995

therapy for overcoming anxiety. While these steps were intended for the treatment of extreme anxiety, they can be applied to less severe manifestations as well. Co-existing with flawed learning within and around us may be gut-wrenching for some, even those not mentally afflicted in any way. Note: Dr Ross's steps have been embellished with additional details in this book.

## SIX STEPS TO MANAGE FEAR

Step 1. Expect, allow, and accept that fear will arise.

At the outset, do not be surprised when you feel fear. Fear is an emotion that needs to be managed, not conquered. Fear happens. We must accept this. This is because the flawed historical basis seems to be woven into our very beings, as instinct; perhaps it is also in our genes. There is no need to tackle fear by overcorrecting it with reckless disregard. As a first step, feeling fear, momentary or otherwise, is to be taken as a given.

Step 2. When fear comes, stop, wait, and refocus.

Some simple focus mechanisms are counting backwards, in pre-determined even or uneven reductions (of 3, 6, 7, for example). Count backward from 100, saying mentally 100…97…94…91… etc. An alternative is to count upward, replacing multiples of five with "fizz" and seven with "buzz" (1, 2, 3, 4, fizz, 6, buzz, 8, 9, fizz…etc. For multiples of both, such as 35, use any one). You can also cope by feeling solid surfaces of different textures. Feel the arm of the chair, the fabric of your dress, the wall behind you, etc. A popular method, used to get over bad habits, is to wear a rubber band around your wrist. You can snap the rubber band on the inside of your wrist until the fear starts subsiding. Such remedies can be continued until the fear reduces to a more manageable level.

Step 3. Focus on doing manageable things in the present, and then build a sharper focus for more complex tasks.

This just means *move*. Don't be like a rabbit or a deer immobilised by the headlights of a car. Do some manageable things. Some manageable things could be just listening, reading, taking notes, drinking water, working out, making a sandwich, etc. Anything appropriate to the current situation, at the level of effectiveness the condition allows. By doing this you prevent yourself from sinking deeper into the fear. You can go on to complex tasks following the next step.

Step 4. Rate your level of fear from zero to ten. Watch it go up and down.

This is a power step for controlling fear. When you do this with concentration, the results will surprise you. You can do this while you are responding to the fear as in Step 3, which is, doing manageable tasks. Ask yourself *What is the level of fear I am feeling right now?* Zero is calmness and serenity; ten is the absolute opposite— uncontrolled panic. Ten is the worst nightmare of what can happen to us or what we can do. Rate the level of fear on a scale of zero to ten and compare it with the situation. As you measure it, you will feel the level of your fear changing. Never mind—keep measuring the level of fear. Now I am feeling a fear-level of six…now five…now it has gone up to seven…down to four…and so on. What this exercise does is kind of amazing. You will find that you are never out of control as far as 'fear' is concerned. The fear will go up and down as you keep giving it a measure, and you should soon be able to get a controllable fix on it. Be assured, it would never reach a ten, on this scale.

Step 5. Function with fear. Appreciate your achievement.

One should practise continuing tasks while being afraid. The steps above should not require a break in activity. To the extent feasible, you need not suspend current tasks to engage in *fear management*. Learn to feel good about the smallest tasks that you achieve while feeling fear. You might have read a little, or you might have exercised, or you might have made yourself that sandwich you deserve... whatever. Just appreciate whatever little you are able to do. As your fears drop off, you will accomplish more.

Step 6. The final step. Expect, allow, and accept that fear will reappear.

This is just step one said another way. Fear is not a feeling that one can leave behind. It is a natural mechanism. It has to be managed and annulled, repeatedly. Accept this as inevitable. Even your reaction to experiencing fear will change as you stop thinking *why am I feeling afraid now*. You know it is okay to feel fear and that you just need to manage it. You will not be surprised the next time you are afraid. The six-step process can be set in motion as necessary.

Some of us would never need to use this tool. Nevertheless, when confronting fear for any reason, or even no reason, it can be reassuring to know that one has it. Apply the technique when you are afraid. You will see its effectiveness.

# GLP 2

# THE ARCHIVED ANXIETY

*A*s explored early in the book, primal therapists first postulated that the trauma of birth affects us. 'A fractured primal integrity from a painful birth experience and unfulfilled primal needs may lead to a person's inability to live consciously and function fully without impairment[53].' The trauma that we carry might have caused us to do some things, early on in our lives, which now are internal obstacles to our progress. Often introversion, aloofness, timidity, meekness and isolation, have their roots in trauma in the womb or may be caused by pain early in life from factors like colic.

One of the best ways to remove these hurdles is healing confrontations with our own recollection of the past, through writing out our history. The following is a

---

[53] Stettbacher, Konrad J, *Making Sense of Suffering: the Healing Confrontation with Your Own Past*. New York, N.Y., U.S.A. Meridian, 1993

summary of a method primal therapists have tested. It is recommended if you feel a need, but with a caution. In primal therapy, *writing out your history* is intended to be a precursor to professional help. Nonetheless, it has proved helpful to just sit at a computer and capture recollections of the past. Using pen and paper may be cumbersome for this process, but use whatever is comfortable for you. This writing might require a few hours over some days, away from your usual routine. If you manage your time well, you would be able to complete this process in a few sittings.

The simplest way to achieve an enhanced level of personal integration is to write out one's own history, as an advocate of the child you were. I suggest that you write the record at least until fourteen years of age, though I found continuing it to later years as also helpful. Feel free to confront people in the past, perhaps in imaginary dialogues, while writing your history. Ask without false pride, as a child would. Feel free to justify the actions of the child within, who could have been carrying a historical load—such as the trauma of childbirth. Some recollections may be painful. If you have painful recollections, it would be best to resolve them, and not shy away from them. Be brave. Describe what you felt or feel now as you write. It just takes effort on your part. Try it and see.

To help you in the exercise, make two lists. First, a list of people you cannot forget because of how they influenced or affected you. Second, a list of events you cannot forget: Events that others made happen and things you did that disturb you even today. With these lists ready, start writing your history in chronological order (as far as possible), and to the extent you remember. Write a telling commentary protecting yourself. Be your own lawyer. In all probability, you were caught in the historical web, and are unaccountable.

In most cases, it is likely to be issues of communication that have caused your lapses, if any. Something you left untold, or failed to do, something misunderstood, or some abnormal behaviour. Also, look at the other side of the coin. Ask for forgiveness from others, and seek restitution where it is needed. Learn to forgive others and yourself—all in your mind and in your writing. Keep doing this, rewriting, enhancing, until you reach a relatively more comfortable present.

The important thing about this exercise is not really the writing, but the constant *rewriting*. You should write, rewrite, and make corrections and changes to your narration and the feelings captured. As you write this history, fortify the case for your old, immature self. This does not mean we change facts. We just change our arguments, explanations, and reactions to our recollections. Do this as often as required. This is why a computer is helpful. It is not surprising to discover a sense of outrage, intimidation, anger, or sheepishness when we keep rereading and rewriting. Every time we revisit and refine this history of ours, we discover a little more about ourselves. We can learn to forgive ourselves, or others, as we resolve those long-standing conflicts within. With some patience, at some point, you will feel released from the damaging thoughts, words and events in your past.

This exercise might be difficult if your circumstances have not changed. That is, if what you want to forget is still in front of you. However, this exercise does free one of several limiting factors of the past. It could be the first time that you sat down and confronted the past. We may never realise how far-reaching the impact of the past is until we articulate its events. When we keep revisiting the articulation, we discover our point of view in it. We discover that we deserve to be free. On some matters that remain unchanged, we may discover we have to start over. If you have assimilated the concepts in this book so far, you will see that this starting over is nothing but a change in perspective. This perspective can be rooted in our personal purpose, measure for measure, as we live life.

I can state only my personal experience, and the success of others in my immediate circle with history-writing. This is an initial step, under the controlled settings of primal therapy, in both the Janov and Stettbacher schools of Primal Therapy. Dr Janov has stated the dangers of *self-primalling*. Nonetheless, the utility of history-writing as an insightful and strengthening exercise was evident to me. I did experience some extreme emotions that I felt were cathartic, but such emotions may not be tolerable for some. Hence, caution is advised. At the very least, you will know if you need professional help, or you will come out with a greatly resolved past. You win either way.

Please note however, if you come across extreme uncontrollable emotions, it is better to seek professional help. If some memories are extremely painful, this is an indication that you have deep-set problems. Stop the effort at once. You should seek professional help. Keep in mind that the idea is to benefit from the exercise and resolve issues, not regress.

# FORGIVE TO FORGET

**A**ll of us have collected some mental baggage. This sometimes blocks us from reasonableness and recovery. It might be as important for us to forget some things or allow them to fade, as it is to forgive others and ourselves. It may be difficult to resolve some memories using the 'history-writing' method. These events keep popping up periodically in our mind in response to some triggers, and sometimes spontaneously. Science claims that there are *physical* traces of memory imprinted in our brains. Memory is dependent on four things:

- The intensity of the impression
- The number of times the event was repeated
- The interest in the event at the time
- The repetition of conditions similar to that in which the memory was formed.

It is possible to minimise the impact of memory, and make it a non-issue eventually. As soon as an unpleasant memory arises, follow it up with the conscious recall of another unrelated event, *even an unpleasant one*, comparable in intensity. This seems a strange response, but it creates interference with the earlier spontaneous memory. You can alternate among these and more such memories consciously, and this will cause a reduction in the intensity of *all* unpleasant memories. When we do this, repetitive flip-flopping among memories, we can come to the present, lessening the impact of negative recollection. The technique consciously uses two or more harsh events in the past, or also significant positive events, to interfere with the moment of unpleasant recall.

Turning highly disturbing memories into harmless forces is feasible with some practise. Try it. The memories of several unpleasant encounters could crop up randomly. Flag each one as a tool for helping to reduce the intensity of another. When you think of one *faux pas*, voluntarily think of another, and perhaps another. Keep flip-flopping among these. The key is to be conscious and recall the interfering memories by volition. You must recognise it as a choice rather than a reaction to depression. This means you remain aware and in control throughout the process, and do not feed a depressive state. Unusual as this may seem, it works. Try it.

You might want to also try a technique for those annoying memories of things you have done or missed—the minor gaffes, the irritants, the missed opportunities, etc. Memory interference is for the strong unpleasant memories, whereas this is for a milder class. The technique combines *history-writing* and *memory-interference*. It involves keeping a small flipbook that you can carry with you. Nowadays, you get flipbooks that fit in a wallet. Write down a title for every annoying memory you can recall in the flipbook—just one or two words for each specific memory, by which you can identify them. Then, when a disturbing memory crops up randomly, open the flipbook and glance through your entire list quickly. You can set in motion a relieving remission of any disturbing memory by just going through your list. Soon it will only be an item in your little book, and not a struggle in the mind. Incidentally, you can keep up your list as you live your life. It is a good teacher.

One thing to remember from our explorations so far is all this *had to happen*. Do not get into wallowing in the past, and be willing to take control from this point forward. It would be as important to stop garnering bad memories, as it is to defuse any unpleasantness of the past. To forget things we accidentally do, there are four things recommended by Geoffrey A. Dudley, a self-help author, from his secondary research on memory[54].

1.  Do not sleep with an unpleasant experience. Keep awake. Just put in the hours.
2.  Do not allow the impression to settle. Distract the mind with a movie or an engrossing book, or company. The more active we are in the interval following the event, the more likely we are to forget.

---

[54]    Dudley, Geoffrey: *Double Your Learning Power*. Northhampton-shire: Thorsons Publishers, 1986.

3. The more similar your activity (in Item 2) following the unpleasant experience is to the experience itself; the easier the unpleasant experience will be to forget. This time, we have to be in sufficient control to choose the subsequent activity and make it a positive one.
4. Trust time to heal.

# GLP 4

## FIND GOLD IN OLD

We very often look at old age as something that happens to someone else. The finality of being in the 'old' bracket of life can be a surprise, or yet another role we slip into comfortably. How we accept ageing can change our lives. A lot has to do with managing the expectations we had for ourselves, and the expectations others have of us. Writing out our history and practising memory-interference techniques could be necessary, but may not be sufficient for some with a mental block. The block makes them feel they are too old to make changes. This chapter highlights two techniques that can be applied by anybody who does not feel adequately detached, regardless of age. They are easy to implement and can help anyone mature emotionally.

Meditation and book-dipping are two very important good living practices when you grow older. A little step back, a little introspection, a little meditation, a little contemplation, and we are likely to become calmer. Meditation has several techniques, and one of the best among them is to observe breathing and the mind in tandem. With some practise, we can keep the observer in us detached and calm any erratic thought stream. We could also chant a non-associative, all encompassing, symbolic representation of our choice, such as *OM* [55] or *Nam-Myo-Ho-Rengey-Kyo*[56] as an aid. The technique is less important than the purpose. The purpose is to get a sense of detachment from the mind's incessant chatter, to be an observer of our thoughts, and calm our thought stream.

Observe your mind when you chant. Soon you will hear the intelligence in you discount those things that do not matter, or cannot matter, in favour of things that do. The wisdom that is your natural state will allow you to ripen as on a vine, until you become detached. You may get random, yet profound ideas, which typically get more and more insightful when you meditate effectively. This will heighten your tendency to become involved with the mind and the thought stream. You *can* follow such thoughts to resolve any inconsistency in your insights, or to remove any conflict in your understanding. But get

---

[55]  *Om* is the mystical sound that represents the source and entirety of creation for the Hindus. It is the basis for what can be called the 'gross' universe, the 'subtle' universe and the 'causal' universe.

[56]  This is the chant of the followers of Nichirin Buddhism. Myo-Ho-Rengey-Kyo is the name of the Lotus Sutra, in Japanese pronunciation of classical Chinese characters. The literal meaning of Nam-Myo-Ho-Rengey-Kyo is 'I devote myself to the Lotus Sutra.'

back to chanting and meditation, observing thoughts, and not feeling fear, even if the contemplative thread is lost in a specific sitting.

The second method, book-dipping, refers to picking up a new or forgotten reflective book, opening it randomly and reading a few lines or paragraphs. If it is a truly reflective book, you will find ideas in it that are relevant to your state of mind—whatever it is, and whichever page you open. To a mind that is receptive, everything is progressive. This happens as we mature, and become active seekers of learning. It is synchronicity of a constructive nature. You will find one or two threads to follow that are relevant to your present cognitive needs. Book-dipping sometimes sets the stage for meditation[57]. You will feel inspired to contemplate the ideas presented. As you contemplate ideas that are appealing to you, peace will follow.

✳ ✳ ✳

Being bold and attempting new techniques that pose no danger will be rewarding, and will aid in the discovery of which techniques work for you. Some have found remarkable growth with the practise of techniques such as Tai Chi. Others take up social or legal issues that were dear to their hearts, but for which they never found the time. Still others find it rewarding to share the knowledge gained from their experiences by writing,

---

[57]    Some mental health researchers are of the opinion that meditation for recovering schizophrenia patients is not advisable. If you do not find meditating relaxing after trying it for a while, and if you feel a persistent anxiety when you attempt to meditate, do not adopt this technique.

lecturing or *satsang*[58]. Socialising and volunteering are also good ways to keep the brain stimulated.

In speaking on a topic similar to the art of growing old gracefully, N. B. Hardeman (1874–1965), an educator, debater and preacher stated, 'I am too young to speak as one should on this subject,' while he was definitely over eighty at the time! Learning to be confident in your uniqueness, whatever your age, is feasible. Three key factors predicting strong mental function in old age are regular physical activity, a strong social support system, and a belief in one's ability to handle what life has to offer.

Judith Heyworth, M.D., the Medical Director and a geriatrician at Advocate Health Center, Sykes, offers this advice. 'As you grow older, you will face challenges and losses. My patients who seem to do the best mentally and physically are those who keep a positive attitude.' A good attitude helps you cope with life's vicissitudes, and this is true for people of all ages. Medical authorities also say laughter is one of the best medicines for the elderly. You can always keep your sense of humour tuned up by surrounding yourself with pleasant and interesting people. Just act your age and do not be afraid to laugh at yourself even when someone else is around.

✳ ✳ ✳

Having said all this, just a few methods or platitudes cannot ameliorate the challenge of old age. As the saying

---

[58]   A Sanskrit word for being in the company of an assembly of persons who listen to, talk about, and assimilate knowledge in search of the highest truth.

goes, 'Old age is not for sissies.' Use the information and techniques in the book, to the fullest extent possible. Go out and grab life, in whatever capacity you can. You can be sure the innately progressive core in you will see you through safely, all your life. Chances are you would get to feel fuller and more confident as you age…

# GLP 5

## BEGINNING TO START OVER

How can we talk of personal purpose when suffering the loss of a loved one? The good living practices for handling grief and heartbreak that follow are only a token of thought. No one can give you a shortcut when it comes to loss. No book can ever replace what you have lost. You could find books that may help, but what you learn from this ultimate challenge is again yours and yours alone. Treat the little learnings and the earth-shaking ones preciously.

* * *

GRIEF: Grief is an issue that we should let slip into the past. Intellectual acceptance that it cannot be any other way may need to precede emotional reconciliation. It is best to remember the difference we explored, between destiny and fate. Death seems to be an aspect of fate, not destiny. Understanding death is in some way, assimilating and accepting life[59]. Life is as much a mystery as death. Hence, despite its idealistic tone, we should try and accept death in the same manner as living. Given its mystery, it is inevitable that solace, if sought, is found only in theology. The best alternative to theological explanations I have come across is from a comment of a child, about six years old. He rationalised loss in a special way. He said, 'People die to make room for babies (!).'

But then, how can we manage the loss if it is the death of a child? Here is where theology can help. Hinduism and Buddhism suggest that early death occurs when an advanced soul reincarnates. When a soul is close to being freed from the bondage of birth and rebirth, it takes birth and lives for a short period. It has a very small amount of *karma* to work out, and this short span of living allows it to do so. Most other religions suggest that god loved the soul of the departed so much, that he could not wait to have him or her back.

When one loses someone dear to the ultimate deadline, it is an unparalleled lesson in personal growth that is forced on us. We must learn to appreciate good memories, and keep building as many new good ones as we can, as quickly as we can. We need to work out our grief and not let it overwhelm us. You must see the fact that you have outlived the departed as a blessing through which you have saved them extreme pain had you preceded them; that their death was brought about by a compassion of an invisible hand, saving them from possible pain and suffering had they lived.

---

[59]    As further reading, McWilliams, Peter, and Harold Bloomfield: *How to Survive the Loss of a Love*. Prelude Press, 1993.

We must allow grief to work itself out in a personally meaningful way. A method similar to writing out one's history can help overcome grief. We can sometimes assuage our grieving by writing a letter to the departed. Write in a personal diary or on a computer, and pour the anger, love, frustration, and all the other feelings induced by the loss into it. In Table 3 is a brief guideline on what you can write about. You could find other meaningful ways that may help in dealing with the loss. Examples are, carrying out an activity dear to the person lost, as homage, or, closing out any vision they would have liked make a reality. Once you have done this letter-writing and/or homage, be sure to only look forward.

Table 3. STATEMENTS TO HELP BUILD A LETTER TO THE DEPARTED

- I admire you because…
- I should have done with you  < all this > …
- If I meet you again, I will…
- I miss you because…
- I should have told you…
- I am sorry for…
- I dedicate to you  < all this >

Please also understand that each of us is unique. There never was a person like the departed and there never will be one like him or her. However, if you accept your uniqueness, you too can look forward, without depending on someone else alone. You need to overcome any defeatist urges, such as the anger or temporary masochism that grief may bring. The departed would want you to be happy. The departed would want to save you your pain. The departed would want you to move on. Cherish the memories you have of them.

In the midst of this great sadness, we may think nothing can make good this loss. This may be true. Perhaps, we cannot volitionally overcome the loss, or conquer the grief, or replace the love. But please don't punish yourself. Shy away from being dramatically tragic or from building unpleasant memories. Even as you cherish the memories of the departed, try to gravitate towards activities that will allow you to grow, and give you a purpose. Be caring and compassionate towards yourself. You deserve it, however horrendous you feel the circumstances are. Appreciate life, however obscure its purpose appears to be.

✳ ✳ ✳

HEARTBREAK: You could have felt a pain similar to grief—heartbreak. We generally experience heartbreak when we are young. The youthfulness need not be in years, but in emotional maturity. The 'object of our affection' often becomes perfect to us, whatever be the footing on which the relationship started. We could have started out thinking, *this is the best thing that ever happened to me*, or maybe just *let's see how it goes*, or even *this will do for now*. The heart invariably idealises what it loves. Heartbreak is almost inevitable when we idealise and then lose the person.

One way to overcome heartbreak is to discover the 'opportunity cost' of relationships. This means discovering the things you are now free to do that you could not do before. One has to think *release* rather than *loss*. An examination of one's life, sometime after the heartbreak, would give reasons, however obscure, for a life without the lost person.

To have loved and lost is usually a foundation to love better than ever before. When you depend totally on another for your confidence, you are likely to discover that unconditional care and compassion are only in storybooks or the movies. Recognise that love is more than a focus between you and another. Love is bigger than you and me, so we cannot conclude we have a monopoly, and disregard everyone else.

One of the best preventions for heartbreak is not to idealise, but to broaden our perspective. We need to acknowledge that no one or no relationship can be eternally or constantly perfect, and that it need not even be so to qualify as successful. The past is not perfect and the future is always promising, without having to be perfect. Move on.

Peter McWilliams (1949–2000) and Dr Harold Bloomfield[60] provide the following pointers in their book, *Overcoming the Loss of a Love* (Table 4 - Points to Help Us Move On). These can help tackle the emotional weight of parting from another. With some licence, these can be applied to parting from another while alive, (heartbreak) and the permanent parting by death (grief):

---

[60]    Harold Bloomfield, MD, is an adjunct professor of psychology at Union Graduate School with a private consultation and psychotherapy practice in Del Mar, Calif.

TABLE 4. Points to Help Us Move On

---

- To forgive does not just mean to pardon, it means to let go.
- Jesus, probably the greatest teacher of forgiveness in history ['Forgive them, Father, for they know not what they do'], used the Aramaic word *shaw,* when he spoke of forgiveness. *Shaw* means, 'to untie.'
- If you are tied to a rock that is pulling you down in the water, all you have to do is *forgive it* (untie it) and swim toward the light.
- When you forgive the past, you untie yourself from the past, and you are free.
- To forgive also means to be *for* (in favour of) *giving* (to deliver a gift). When you forgive, you affirm that you are in favour of giving.
- To whom do you give? Another? Sometimes. Yourself? Always. When you release another to go their way, you free yourself to do the same. The process of giving oneself this gift of freedom is forgiveness

---

The waiting may be hard, but one can trust time to heal. Time will cradle you in its natural cycle. It is benevolent even as it is demanding. Life, more often than not, will provide strength, even as it tests it. Look forward… Look outward… Reach out and you will be pleasantly surprised at the way life helps. Life lives. Take courage.

# GLP 6

## THE LAST ERROR

ou would have assimilated the discussions and techniques so far, but there could still be one hurdle—your habitual negative thoughts. Why do you have disturbing thoughts although you understand there is no need to be disturbed? To go beyond intellectual understanding to emotional maturity, first step back, and away from disturbing thoughts by checking to see if you are committing an error in your thinking[61]. The last error is really error in thinking; continuing to think in the same manner as in

---

[61] This 'last mile' is based on the path-breaking work of Dr Aaron Beck. Dr Beck is professor emeritus in the department of psychiatry at the University of Pennsylvania. He is regarded as the father of cognitive therapy, and his pioneering theories are widely used in the treatment of clinical depression. This is a short-list of some ideas derived from his work, but with some embellishments. I have attempted, to the best of my ability, not to underplay or misconstrue Dr Beck's original work. I apologise for any shortfall in articulation and take full responsibility for any errors.

the past, despite having progressive ideas. In spite of our understanding, deep-set discouraging beliefs may keep replaying in our minds. To handle these, become conscious of the type of error in your thinking.

Flag any unhelpful or disturbing thought you have into one of the following ten types and discard or challenge it. Pause and become conscious of the possible errors in thinking. Just classifying the thought into the types below will free enough energy to be proactive...

## Are you...

1. **Predicting the future?** The future is always yet to happen. Do not predict it in your thinking. Do not indulge in negative imaging.

2. **Jumping to conclusions?** So what if a person you know did not say hello when you saw him or her in public. There may have been a million things going through the person's mind. Do not jump to conclusions based on superficial observations. You cannot conclude negatively from an event that could be random. Do not overdo it in your imagination.

3. **Over-generalising?** Just because something happened in a particular way in the past, does not mean it will happen the same way now. Do not make the mistake of discerning a negative pattern when there is none. Give it a rest.

4. **Focusing on the negative?** Every dark cloud has a silver lining. Learn to recognise it. Every story has two sides. Do not just read one. Look for the positive facts if you do not want to feel miserable.

Granted, some events tend to drag us down, but that is temporary. Take control and absorb that which is constructive and can be helpful to you.

5. **Focusing on Weakness?** Okay, so you have some weaknesses. However, do not forget your strengths. Cast away that focus on your weakness. Cannot concentrate now? No sweat! You'll get it right eventually. You don't have a very disciplined or organised schedule. Not a problem! Perhaps you need to do this spontaneously. You *have* a purpose, and can discover the ability to do just what you are supposed to do. Do not dwell on your weaknesses.

6. **Thinking in extremes?** Life is not black and white, but shades of grey. It is not all good, or all bad, but a mix of both. Become conscious of thinking in extremes. See the grey instead of just black and white. In every situation, every person, and every incident, there are degrees of good and bad. It is not just good *or* bad, even if it might seem so at that moment. There is no need to get totally euphoric or completely dismayed.

7. **Expecting perfection?** If you have been expecting perfection from yourself, it is time to wake up. A perfect 10 is an Olympic score. A few of us *are* equipped to get a perfect score in figure skating. However, all of us, including our Olympian champions, need not apply such a measure to everyday life. Let the facts of your effort speak. If your intent is correct, you will be able to accept the result, and commit to keep getting better or to improve. On some issues,

you may even recognise a point of diminishing returns... where the effort you need put in outweighs the improvement you can make.

8. **Self-blaming?** If things go wrong, do not take all the blame. Several things contribute to success and failure. There always are mitigating circumstances. If you are thinking you alone are to blame, it is time to flag that thought. Remember the 'Uncertainty' model and Karma. Many factors form the results. Disconnect from any masochistic need that prompts you to punish yourself.

9. **Reasoning emotionally?** Do not think you know what others feel just because of the way you are feeling. You are an island of emotion. Nobody caught that slight tremor in your voice during your last stage performance. You think in private. Do not assume others have a hotline to your emotions. Do not reason that other's actions are a result of your internal emotions of the moment.

10. **Thinking about or blaming the past?** Focus on the present. The past is where it belongs. It does not matter at what stage in life you are or how deep you are into an interaction. Your worries about the past and its impact can be converted to learning. MOVE ON. If you are alive, there is a tomorrow. Your mission is not complete. If you have difficulty disengaging from the past, try the history-writing and memory-interference techniques explored earlier.

You should challenge every disturbing thought that comes into your mind. Practise stepping back and categorising disturbing or unhelpful thoughts into the 10 types discussed. *The very act of doing this is important.* This act is a progressive step, which interrupts the harmful flow. The classification of the errors in thinking is a simple, yet effective technique. It does not demand that you fool yourself with positive fantastic thoughts, but only that you deny defeatist thinking.

You would find it easier to apply the technique by carrying a small card with titles of these ten points written on it. When you feel disturbed, fish out the card and weigh any uneasy thoughts you have against the list. After some practice, you will be able to refocus your thoughts, and manage the mind's chatter. With some effort, you will find you are able to manage a wild mind. You will soon transform yourself into a confident thinker.

In closing, if you habitually feel uneasy or in a bind, discount it by recollecting some things you find fulfilling, or some things good about yourself. Think of a few uplifting things like a pet welcoming you home, the laughter of an infant or even 'raindrops on roses and whiskers on kittens.[62]' When you think you are undeserving, say to yourself 'I deserve what life has to offer me.' When you feel your inner calm disturbed, say to yourself, 'Relax, this will also pass.' When someone knocks down your work with destructive criticism, say to yourself, 'I am getting better and better each day'. There are three kinds of self-assurances you can give yourself that should help to counter discouraging thinking.

---

[62]    From the song "Favourite Things" in the classic film *Sound of Music* (1965)

1. I believe in myself (in my skills, my temperament, etc.)
2. I deserve the good things (leisure, compliments, etc.)
3. I am getting better every day (improving, getting wiser, etc.)

Say these things and their variants to yourself as if you do not have a care in the world. Then constructive change will happen, steadily. The way you see yourself, the way people see you, and the things you do will take on an aura of excellence. The change will happen in 'real time' as you learn to keep being proactive in every moment. Soon you will be poised, even in severely challenging situations.

✳ ✳ ✳

The last of the good living practices or heuristics have been shared. You can build the ability to mitigate any fringe symptoms and negativity just by your practise of the GLPs. If you have been reading the hypotheses and applying the heuristics covered, you are probably more in control. If this is not the case, stop and check to see if you are having the symptoms of any disability. You may need professional help to enhance the effectiveness of the information we have just been through. Don't attach any stigma to reaching out. It is in you to get real, build confidently and look ahead. It is never ever too late. Trust life and life will trust you. Get started now!

# EPILOGUE

There is a tacit assumption in the book that medication can work across a broad spectrum of those afflicted. The fact is, for as many patients for whom medication works, there is an equal, if not greater number for whom it doesn't. It is therefore important to recognise that it is, usually, the perspective that one is a survivor and not a victim that helps, rather than medication alone. There is a case to see symptoms, like hallucinations and delusions, as consequences of early trauma to the self. Perhaps it is our psyche trying to resolve itself by presenting such manifestations. If so, it must be our ability to work collaboratively with these manifestations, instead of feeling victimised, that will eventually help us.

I reproduce the following tenets of the Hearing Voices Movement, a movement devoted to demystify and remove the stigma attached to such symptoms.

- Hearing voices is a common human experience which, although it can cause distress, is not in itself a symptom of illness.
- Distressing voices can be metaphors for problems in the hearer's life.
- The voices can be resolved by addressing the underlying emotions and conflicts that they represent.

These are quoted verbatim from Eleanor Longden's e-book. *Learning from the Voices in My Head* (TED Books) (Kindle Locations 1022-1024). TED Conferences. Kindle Edition. She provides helpful information and tips on how to confront, cope and collaborate with such manifestations in the same book.

All of us, while not free of problems, have the ability to focus on our blessings. We can accept that we cannot change what we cannot influence, and, drive what we *can* influence with gusto. Our security is not affected by what we possess or do not possess, and is based instead on a confidence in our abilities. We can understand there will be enough air to last us until our last breath, and have the faith that the rest will also be there.

Whether you have faith in a universal force or not, there is a guiding energy leading us towards whatever we believe. If this belief is constructive and reflects confidence, progressive things happen. If our beliefs are destructive or defeatist, negative emotions like fear, guilt, aggression and resentment would hold their sway. But, if we take small steps towards becoming proactive and confident consistently, we change gradually at the core of our beings. We attract the forces that keep making us better. Personal, yet purposeful direction has a self-multiplying effect.

You grow inexorably with time; hence, progress you will. If we go about the business of life, focusing on bettering our state of mind every day, we evolve. This evolution is a natural consequence of time, and does not contradict the journey of the species. As we move in our slice of time, put all what has happened, this book too, behind you. All that has happened can be a foundation for new ventures from this point forward. It is likely that you have strengthened the foundations themselves, whatever their state prior to our explorations. Now build boldly. Live out the rest of your life, whatever the number of days (or minutes!) with caring, and without fear or malice.

To be human is to care. Care for *yourself* and others. To care is the starting point of responsible living. We then travel through the understanding of many paradigms, none of which may ever be, or indeed *needs* to ever be complete. There will always be gaps. It is meant to be this way. This is the way the cosmos maintains our *independent interdependence*. If we desire an ultimate goal and grace, we may need to understand we already have it. Just choose, discover, and take care to be the *human* you really are; all that could be 'God' will take care of the rest.

# MORE HELP?

*n*othing worthwhile comes without effort. It takes patience to build oneself back into the mainstream. One has to learn how to shift from a sense of being victim to a survivor, step-by-step. When you have the intent to turn things around, and are ready to make the effort, things can change.

I offer Patient-to-patient (P2P) counselling out of a clinic in Chennai, India, for people who are responding to medication, and want to come back to the mainstream. In these interactions, besides the 6 GLPs, I help you to accept where you are currently, and also help you in starting afresh, with confidence and poise.

I may be able to help. But eventually, it needs you to pick-up yourself up by the boot-straps. I am ready if you are ☺

If you are a care-giver, I may be able to give you an insight into the workings of the mind of an afflicted ward, and hopefully help you empathise with patients having the condition.

You can get in touch with me at the following email. I will receive your request and respond as quickly as possible.

ganesh.i.me.us@gmail.com

Wish you wellness,
Ganesh N Rajan

# A little bit of history and a lot of thank yous

My first child was born in 1994. The doctor assured my wife and me that he was a hundred per cent normal. But, you know how it is with first-time parents. My questions, on what could go wrong, would not stop. The doctor then began interrogating me about my health and that of my spouse. In retrospect, the doctor was probably trying to dismiss me, as her professional opinion that everything was okay just did not deter me. When I mentioned schizophrenia, she said, though not fully validated, the offspring of afflicted persons may have a slightly increased chance of developing schizophrenia. That is, everyone has a random chance of one per cent, and my son, *perhaps* a tiny fraction more. Right then, despite the minuscule chance of its occurrence, I decided that I must educate my son (and subsequently, daughter) on this condition.

I searched for a book that would explain what I had experienced. I wanted a book that included lessons for the *normal*. I couldn't find any. I therefore did the next best thing and wrote some notes for my children to read. The book you have just read is a metamorphosis of those notes over about fifteen years.

Many people helped in the development of this book and I profess my appreciation and thanks to them. Firstly, three people in my immature past, for showing me how twisted reality can be, and who will remain anonymous in deference to the fact that all of us have moved on. Secondly, Swami Dayanandaji, for leading me to the ideas, which helped me to a new beginning.

Finally, for constructive and corrective inputs, or for assistance in the book taking its final shape and reaching you, the following, in chronological order of their help: Susan (Gita), Khandadi, Mr. Seshan, Shanker, (Late) Mr. Ganapathy, Ramnarayan, Gayathri, Yathiraj, Ranjini, Dr Tharoor, Geetha, Shivalingappa, Jo (Jyothi), Mrs. Shastri, Dr Mohan, Dr Samuel, Vatsala, Arun, Col. Ajay, Ankush, Sanjana, Mr. Bhanu, Suresh, Arvind, Kishore, Anand, Mr. Jayaraman, Jaishanker, Tommy (Prakash), Gautam, Prita, Sanghamitra, Shrutika, Sudha, Krishna Kumar, Vipin and Rahul.

And of course, I thank you, my reader! I hope this book has helped you towards rejoicing in yourself... enduringly—GNR

9 789385 152139